MURFREESBORO
IN THE
CIVIL WAR

MURFREESBORO
IN THE
CIVIL WAR

MICHAEL R. BRADLEY
AND SHIRLEY FARRIS JONES

THE
History
PRESS

Published by The History Press
Charleston, SC 29403
www.historypress.net

First published 2012

ISBN 978.1.54023.099.7

Library of Congress Cataloging-in-Publication Data

Jones, Shirley Farris.
Murfreesboro in the Civil War / Shirley Farris Jones and Michael R. Bradley.
p. cm.
Includes bibliographical references.
ISBN 978-1-60949-459-9
1. Murfreesboro (N.C.)--History--19th century. 2. North Carolina--History--Civil
War, 1861-1865. 3. Murfreesboro (N.C.)--Biography. I. Bradley, Michael R. (Michael
Raymond), 1940- II. Title.
F264.M9J67 2012
975.6'03--dc23
2012002972

This book is most respectfully dedicated as a 150ᵗʰ Anniversary Tribute to Murfreesborough during the Civil War.

To the town—resistant to the point of being "captured" but strong enough to survive the occupation of both Armies.

To her sons and soldiers—who fought valiantly for the cause they believed to be right, whether North or South; who suffered, who bled, who died.

To her citizens—men and women, young and old, black and white, who stayed behind and kept the home fires burning; who possessed the humanity to feed and nurse the wounded of both sides; and who had the courage to pick up the pieces and move forward together into the next century to make us who we are today.

Contents

Acknowledgements

O ur thanks is offered to the many people who have assisted in the research and preparation of this book. We were warmly received by the Albert Gore Research Center at Middle Tennessee State University. Dr. James H. Williams has a wonderful staff for the center led by Mr. James Havron, archivist and coordinator, and ably assisted by Kelsey Fields, graduate assistant. The Gore Center holds a wealth of information about Murfreesboro during the Civil War years. The staff of the History Room at the Linebaugh Public Library in Murfreesboro were always available to assist in tracking down elusive bits and pieces of materials, especially microfilm of newspapers.

At Stones River National Battlefield Park, Mr. Gilbert Backlund, Mr. Jim Lewis and Mr. John R. George all gave freely of their time and knowledge to assist this effort. The staff at Oaklands has been quite gracious in providing photos of the interior and exterior of the house and in answering questions about the visit of Jefferson Davis to the Maney home. Special thanks to Nila Gober at Oaklands for her enthusiastic help.

1
The Storm Clouds Gather

SECESSION CRISIS

The pretty little town of Murfreesboro was barely fifty years old when it became a focal point of the Civil War in the West. From 1811, when the town was founded, until 1861, life in the town had been interesting but hardly dramatic.

From 1818 to 1826, Murfreesboro was the capital of the state, but political maneuvering moved the seat of government elsewhere, and Nashville became the permanent location of state government in 1843. Meanwhile, Murfreesboro was growing. Twenty saloons were open to quench the thirst of residents and visitors, while four hotels served the needs of travelers. Many private homes took in the weary, and all accommodations were usually full when court was in session. By 1830, there was a theater, though the members of the town's numerous churches stayed away from the questionable moral atmosphere of the playhouse. That same year, a stagecoach line linked Murfreesboro with Nashville to the north and with Huntsville, Alabama, far to the south. Education flourished with Bradley Academy, founded in 1809, attracting students such as future president James K. Polk, and Union University, founded in 1823, drawing students from across the entire region. Schools for young ladies included Soule Academy, named for Bishop Soule of the Methodist Church. A cotton factory, a carriage factory, a manufacturer of cedar buckets, a flour mill and similar light industry were stimulated by the construction of the

Nashville & Chattanooga Railroad, whose first cars ran along the new line in 1851. Around the courthouse square were to be found general merchandise stores, two drugstores, a bookstore, jewelry stores, a livery stable and a hardware store. By 1860, there were thirty-five manufacturing concerns in and near Murfreesboro, employing 136 workers, and the town was building a municipal gasworks. The new courthouse (still in use) was completed in 1859 at a cost of $50,000.

Within the city limits, the 1860 census shows a population of 3,861, with 121 of these being listed as slaveholders. This group of citizens held 891 slaves. A few slave owners had as many as a dozen slaves, but many held only 1 or 2. J.B. Palmer, mayor of Murfreesboro from 1855 to 1859 and a future Confederate brigadier, held 9 slaves. Four were male, all minor children; 5 were females, of which one was a minor.[1]

Politically, Murfreesboro had a strong Whig inclination. Nationally, the Whigs favored the use of tax money to support internal improvements such as improving navigation on rivers, having the government construct roads and providing subsidies for railroads. Murfreesboro voters frequently favored the Whig candidates for state and national offices, while local elections were hotly contested and political rallies were popular social occasions. Then came the presidential election of 1860. Murfreesboro Whigs were in a state of disarray. Since 1853, their party had been less and less effective on the national level and had failed to select a candidate for president in 1856. In the North, many Whigs had joined the Republican Party, whose economic views were quite similar to those of the Whigs. In the South, the Republicans were viewed as a sectional party, and the old Whigs did not wish to join them; on the other hand, Murfreesboro Whigs reflected a common view—they had never voted for a Democrat, and they did not intend to do so in 1860. The result was the organization of a new group called the Constitutional Union Party, with Senator John Bell of Tennessee as its standard-bearer. This party proved to be short-lived, but it provided a political home for Tennessee Whigs in 1860.

The Democrats held a convention in Charleston, South Carolina, in the summer of 1860 but failed to nominate a candidate after not being able to agree on a platform position dealing with slavery. Subsequent meetings produced two candidates: Stephen A. Douglas of Illinois and former vice-president John Breckinridge of Kentucky. Bell, Douglas and Breckinridge were the presidential candidates among whom the voters of Murfreesboro, and Tennessee, would choose in November 1860. Abraham Lincoln's name did not appear on the ballot in Tennessee or other Southern states because there was no Republican organization in those states to collect signatures on a qualifying petition.[2]

Beginning in September 1860, the supporters of the various candidates started to promote their men. Former mayor and future Confederate officer J.B. Palmer spoke out for Bell. The editor of the *Murfreesboro News*, G.T. Henderson, wrote in support of Breckenridge.[3] The Democrats made the bigger splash in public events in Murfreesboro. On October 17, a large Breckenridge rally was held on the courthouse square, with the Columbia Blues, the Breckenridge Rangers and the Breckenridge Old Guards militia companies all marching to the venue. The Democratic Ladies of Murfreesboro presented the Breckenridge Old Guards with a banner. After a program of music and speeches, a parade of decorated carriages and wagons led the crowd to a local picnic grove, where hogs had been barbequed.[4]

The supporters of Senator John Bell were not quiescent. A prominent local Whig was James Moore King, a wealthy plantation owner who had fought in the War of 1812 and who was well known for his support of the Union. In a memorandum to himself, King summarized his thoughts on the role and value of the Union:

> *We should adhere to the Constitution as it is. We should continue according to the acts and deeds of the administrations of George Washington, Thomas Jefferson, James Madison, and James Monroe, they have literally defined and explained every section, article, and sentence in the Constitution during their administrations, and by the acts of congress according to the true intent and meaning of that Hallowed document.*

As a good Whig, King expressed support for tariffs to raise the revenue necessary to pay the expenses of the government and to protect both agriculture and industry. He continued:

> *I go for the Union of the states first—I go for the Union of the states last; I go for the Union of the states forever: I go for the Union of the states in politics; I go for the Union of the states to the point of the sword and the sword to the hilt. And DAMNED be them that goes for the disunion of the United States.*

The great fear for King, and for many others of that time, was that if the nation began to separate there would be no end of divisions. Already

John Bell. *Courtesy of the Tennessee State Library and Archives.*

there had been talk of a separate nation in New England in 1814, and the Mormons in Utah had just been forced by the United States Army to submit to anti-polygamy laws passed in Washington. Such continued separation into many small, weak coalitions would leave each one subject to European domination and would spell the end of the quest to achieve the nation's manifest destiny.[5]

Standing behind such views in the heated political atmosphere of Murfreesboro in 1860 was not easy. In the spring of 1861, after Lincoln had been elected and talk of secession filled the air in Tennessee, King went one day to Crockett & Ransom's store on the square to while away some time in conversation with other men. On this occasion, King again declared his unwavering support for the Union only to be approached by a man of forty-five years—a towering six-footer weighing about two hundred pounds and a fire-eating states' rights proponent. "You'll not fight if there is a war because you are for the Union," the man goaded. King, age sixty-nine, took up his hickory walking stick and advanced on the loudmouth. "Damn you, Sir! Try me!" The younger man left the store.[6]

King was outspoken throughout the election campaign. At a political rally at Bomars Mill, the staunch old Whig was asked to offer a toast. He stood and declaimed, "Tennesseans, in principle we are all republicans and Democrats and the offspring of the Whigs of '76 to defend those principles from violation of power and oppression."[7] It should be noted that his use of "republican" is lower case, indicating a set of principles; it is not a proper noun indicating the name of a political party. He uses "Democrats" and "Whigs" as proper nouns.

Whigs also marched through the streets of Murfreesboro singing a campaign song to the tune of *Yankee Doodle*:

Let the North meet with the South
Shake hands in friendly union;
Raise our glorious standard up
Put down all disunion.[8]

Election day brought some sense of finality, if not a sense of relief. Once the votes were counted, options for the future were more clearly defined. The local candidate, John Bell, carried Tennessee with 69,274 votes. Breckenridge placed second, with 64,709, while Douglas was a distant third, polling 11,350 votes.[9] With the Democrats split between Breckenridge and Douglas, and with Bell draining off support in Southern states, it was no surprise that the Republican candidate, Lincoln, won in the Electoral College although carrying only about 40 percent of the popular vote. Almost as soon as the ink was dry on the headlines announcing the election results, the state of South Carolina left the Union, and the local paper endorsed the move, editorializing that "after thirty years of contention and northern efforts to rob the South the time has come to separate peacefully." The *Rutherford Telegraph* did not agree; its editor said, "Under the circumstances which now exist there is no cause whatsoever for separation and he that favors it can be guilty of nothing short of treason to his country."[10]

The governor of Tennessee, Isham Harris, agreed with the disunionists and led the fight to convince the voters of the state to follow the example of the Deep South states, seven of which seceded and sent representatives to Montgomery, Alabama, to form a new government led by Jefferson Davis as president. In February 1861, the issue was put to the test of the ballot, and the results said "no" to secession.[11] By the time Lincoln was sworn in, the Confederacy was a functioning entity with a constitution; national, state and local governments; and armed forces. The only hopeful sign was that Tennessee, and other states in the upper South, had not left the Union. The crisis might still be resolved, many hoped. Then, on April 12, 1861, shots were fired in Charleston, South Carolina, in order to force the U.S. garrison of Fort Sumter to surrender. Lincoln called for seventy-five thousand volunteers to "put down a domestic insurrection," and Isham Harris breathed defiance. Now there was a war; the only decision to be made was which side one was on. June 1861 saw Tennesseans return to the polls to reconsider the secession question. The effect of the fighting was clear in the voting: in every area of the state, the support for secession increased. In Murfreesboro, only seventy-three votes were cast for Union.[12]

Isham Harris. *Courtesy of the Tennessee State Museum.*

16

It was with tears in their eyes but hope in their hearts that residents of Murfreesboro watched on a bright morning in June 1861 as the familiar Stars and Stripes was lowered from the dome of their courthouse. A few minutes later, a new flag rose up the pole, the Stars and Bars of the first national flag of the Confederate States of America. One of those crying was Dr. James Madison Pendleton, pastor of the First Baptist Church. He opposed slavery and supported the Union, but his stand caused him to leave town in October 1862. And as their new flag unfurled in the gentle summer breeze, the good folks of this heretofore quiet little town never dreamed that they would ever hear the roar of cannon, the rattle of musketry or the groans of the dying—much less in their own backyards. It was the opinion of John Cedric Spence, a successful merchant and businessman of Murfreesboro, that anyone choosing to experience the horrors of war would have to "travel hundreds of miles to witness such scenes."[13]

OFF TO WAR

In Murfreesboro, as in so many other towns, both South and North, prominent men put up posters announcing that they were forming companies of troops for service. Now that the decision had been made, even prominent Whigs such as Joseph B. Palmer lent themselves to the war effort. When first seen in his Confederate uniform, a friend asked Palmer, "What does this mean?" Palmer replied, "It means I am doing my duty as going as my people are going."[14] Many men soon came to the county seat and signed the enlistment papers. Companies of about one hundred men each were raised and went to war as Company I, 1st Tennessee; Company A, 2nd Tennessee; Companies C and F, 18th Tennessee; Company E, 20th Tennessee, Company F, 23rd Tennessee; Company A, 24th Tennessee; Companies C, D, E, I and K, 45th Tennessee; Company D, 11th Tennessee Cavalry; and Company D, 21st Tennessee Cavalry. Proportional to their populations, Rutherford County and Murfreesboro became one of the major centers for Confederate support in the entire state. In fact, the area was denuded of men of military age.

After some weeks spent recruiting, the various companies were accepted into service as members of the Provisional Army of Tennessee and made ready to go to a training camp. For the men from Murfreesboro, this destination was Camp Trousdale, some seventy-five miles from their homes, near the town of Portland in Sumner County. On May 2, 1861, the streets were crowded as throngs of citizens watched the local men parade from the square to the depot as the band played the march version of a popular ballad, "Annie Laurie."[15] One of the companies was led by Captain William Ledbetter. His father, William Sr., stayed at home to carry out a contract that the State of Tennessee had given the family business. They had received $7,500 to convert their machine shop to produce Harpers Ferry model rifles for the use of the gathering soldiers.[16] One of the men who was at Camp Trousdale in the regiment commanded by Joseph B. Palmer wrote home soon after arriving:

> *I seat myself upon a pile of straw, blankets, knapsacks, etc. to write you for the first time since leaving home. We arrived at this camp on the R.R. Leading to Clarksville Friday evening, pitched our tents among two or three thousand volunteers and are now spending a real soldiers life. We see nothing scarcely but volunteers and hear nothing but the sound of drums and fife and the noise of camp life. Our camp is pitched about 2 or 3 hundred yards from the main encampment where we are to form another regiment, our company being the first Co. A 4th Reg. I shall now tell you something about our fare, we are divided into messes of 8 men and our provisions are issued out to us. We have bacon, meal or flour, a little rice, potatoes, sugar, coffee and salt and then we can cook to suit ourselves you would have laughed to see me cooking supper this evening with my sleeves rolled up to my elbows and then washing dishes after supper such as tin pans tin cups, we have no spoons, knives nor forks but use our fingers, pocket knives sharp sticks, etc. As to privileges we have scarcely any, we are bound up fast we have a guard placed around our camp which we cannot leave unless we go to the spring for water. The boys think it is hard, but we cannot help it we cannot tell how long we shall stay here at this camp it may be weeks or even months but time alone will tell but as soon as our services are needed we shall be off. I could write you a longer letter but I have no convenient place to write.[17]*

Disease was prevalent at Camp Trousdale. Large numbers of young men with no previous exposure to infectious illnesses, such as measles and mumps, fell sick in large numbers. Often, the best available medical care was unavailing. Funerals in the camp became a familiar sight. On July 1, one soldier wrote from the camp where so many men from Murfreesboro were training:

Today is my time to stand guard and I write your letter during my time to rest. There are fifty eight sick in the Hospital with the measles and many other cantageous [sic] *diseases. One man died last Saturday in Numan's* [Newman's] *regiment, and they buried him yesterday in honor of war. I happened to be over there when they started with him I went to the burying when we got there we found a camp ground surrounded with tombs. The Funeral was preached by a very able minister who is the Chaplain of the regiment, the harbor under which the sermon was preached was about 50 yards from the grave of the warrior and during the sermon I (being tired) layed* [sic] *down to sleep and when I awoke I found myself alone, but ran up to the graveyard and they were just putting him in the grave, they covered the body slightly with dirt and they fired twenty four guns over the grave, which seemed to carry up honor to the God of battle. I would not like to be buried here if I were to die, but would want to be brought home.*[18]

For some of the recruits, death became so familiar that it required but little comment unless the deceased was someone well known to them. John Bradford wrote to his sister:

The health of the camp is tolerably good. There were two deaths up here this week from the measles but I did not understand whose regiment they belonged to. We drill only five hours in the day from 7 o'clock in the morning until 1 and 4½ PM until 6½ and then we get our suppers. We have not drawn our arms yet, but we expect to draw them this week.[19]

Many of the letters home were tinged with youthful pride and naivety, as when James Taft reported, "I have not been sick a single day yet and feel like I could fell ten Yankees by myself." Taft's enthusiasm was tempered by his reaction to the tight discipline the regiment was placed under. "We don't have the privilege of a nigger."[20]

For some, neither pride nor patriotism was enough to sustain the effort of becoming a soldier. The conditions were too challenging, the work too difficult, the discipline too confining and the experience not what had been expected. Some deserted the cause within weeks. Edward Bradford told his mother:

We have the best drilled company in Camp Trousdale, do more work and have less sickness than any company in our regiment [20th Tennessee].

We have had two or three deaths here in the last few days but only one in our regiment. There was a man who died in the Perry Guards last night. There has been two run away, but they caught one of them and drummed him out of the camp. They had one side of his head shaved and a pair of horns on him, his breeches rolled up to his knees, barefooted with his shoes in his hand, his budget [knapsack] *on his back and a board across his back on which was marked "Deserter." He made tracks for Kentucky as soon as he was turned loose...some of the companies have not drawn arms yet. We have a great many ladies to visit us, but I think this is the last place in the world for ladies and I would advise all of connection of that sex to stay at home.*

  P.S. I send you in this five dollars. I want you to get me two Dark Calico Shirts with it and send them up by the first one that comes.[21]

Edward Bradford, and most of his compatriots in the 20th Tennessee, as well as those from the other units with ties to Murfreesboro, acclimated themselves to the military life with surprising speed. Edward wrote to his father:

We are getting plenty to eat and plenty of exercise. We drill two hours twice a day. They carry us about two miles from Camp to drill us and when we get back we have to stay on our own ground, about an acre. We have not been formed into a regiment as yet but will be in a few days. I enjoy everything but the way we sleep. We have not got any straw in our tents and have to sleep on the ground with one blanket to cover with. We have a dance every night. We have more music than we want. There is about a dozen fiddlers to every camp. Brother John and I both had to stand guard last night from eleven until one.[22]

Then, there were the girls they left behind. Sergeant B.P. Bradley, of the 18th Tennessee, wrote to Martha Justice:

Dearest Pet,
I would have given anything if I could have seen you then and enjoyed your sweet smile and have heard your gentle voice, but it could not be so, and sometimes when I think that probably I will never more see you, my heart swells with grief and my eyes swim with tears; but Pet, I will not let such thoughts arise when I can help it for it must be that we will meet again if it is the will of Kind Providence.[23]

Soldier at Camp Trousdale. *Courtesy of the Tennessee State Museum.*

The men who made up the Provisional Army of Tennessee still thought of themselves as free-born citizens of a democracy and, as such, demanded the democratic right to elect those who governed them; they elected their officers. This means time in camp was spent on political maneuvering, as well as learning how to maneuver on the battlefield. Dr. U.G. Owen of the 20th Tennessee wrote home about his fate in that regiment's election:

I was beaten for Asst. Surgeon by one vote, the officers only voted. Prof. A. Winn, Maj Duffy, and Capt. Rucker left their votes and went home but my opponents took that advantage and would not let their votes be put in, that beat me. There is a good deal of excitement about it in the regiment. Some want the election contested because it was thought wrong. The Regiment says that justly I am the choice. Col. Battle says I must have some position in the Army as a surgeon if the war goes on. I have had an offer of a position in the Hospital. I don't know whether I will take it or not.[24]

Finally, the day came for which the men had waited. Weapons were issued, and they began to feel like soldiers sure enough. John Bradford recorded his feelings when writing to his father, "We have drawn our arms which are flint lock muskets and we are learning to drill very fast." Flintlock muskets were poor weapons with which to go to war. Such firearms had been obsolescent since the era of the Mexican War, but Bradford and his unit were not alone in receiving this old-fashioned weapon. Governor Isham Harris received a report from Camp Trousdale that noted that Colonel Fulton's regiment of 889 men received percussion rifles; Colonel Palmer's 883 men, Colonel Savage's 952 men, Colonel Newman's 914 men and Colonel Battle's 880 men all received flintlocks.

The issuing of these obsolete weapons caused more grumbling than any other event at the training camps. However, there was nothing to be done to remedy the situation except make the best of it. It was in this spirit that James Moore King wrote to his sons. Although he had opposed secession, King was one of the many old Whigs who felt that Lincoln's call for troops left him no alternative but to support the Confederate cause. As an old soldier, the father gave sage advice to his sons:

> *I hear complaints about officers being too strict or arrogant. This is no more or less than I would expect. From my own considerable experiences I can tell you that there are good officers and bad officers. In the first place, you should learn to know what your duties are. Then take pride in performing them with energy and dispatch. If you do not know what your duties are they will always be irksome and difficult to perform.*

King goes on to say that military law should be carefully explained to the soldiers by a competent officer. Like all fathers in all ages, King expresses concern for the moral character of his sons given the temptations associated with military life. He advises them to stay away from "harmless mischief" lest that become a slippery slope that would lead to serious troubles.[25]

In Murfreesboro, an activity was beginning that would become very familiar as the war wound on through its course. Young Kate Carney recorded in her diary that

> *the Misses Murfree and Burton came out begging for soldiers. Poor fellows I don't know how any one could refuse them aid. The boxes are going to be sent on to Virginia* [Tennessee had soldiers in that area] *next Tuesday. Ma is going to give them some blankets and pillows, make some salve, and send some rags and lint. I feel sad, for somehow I can't help thinking the first Regt has been in an engagement in West Virginia. I could write many pages about our war and brave soldiers.*[26]

Kate was referring to Maney's 1st Tennessee, which served in Virginia for several months at the beginning of the war before being transferred back to Tennessee. The state of West Virginia did not exist until 1863, and Kate used the term to refer to the western portion of Virginia.

News of the victory at Manassas renewed patriotism for the new nation. A Home Guard to assist the sheriff in maintaining order was formed of men over military age and of boys too young for regular service. A sewing society was established by the townswomen, and a hospital for sick soldiers was set up in the buildings of Union College. The crop came in with a heavy yield, and times seemed good; there was great confidence that the war would not last long.[27]

Only a few days after weapons were issued, Governor Isham Harris officially transferred the troops in the Provisional Army of Tennessee to Confederate control. The men from Murfreesboro were now part of a large organization; they were becoming participants in the big picture. A transformative event had just taken place in the lives of these individuals and in the life of the community, of the state and of the nation. None would ever be the same again.

The Storm Breaks in Murfreesboro

CLOUDS GATHER

The winter of 1861–62 was rather quiet in Murfreesboro. Some soldiers who became ill while in transit on the Nashville & Chattanooga Railroad were taken from the trains and moved to the Confederate hospital in the buildings of Union University. Letters arrived from the various camps telling of life with the army—mostly news of boredom and a wish for home cooking, and occasionally news of fighting. The diary of John C. Spence records that

> *nothing of importance has transpired of late, but still an anxiety in the minds of the people of what would next take place. The purchase of goods had stopped some time since by the merchants that were in the habit of getting supplies from the North. Our carriage shops were in the manufacture of ambulances, wagons, and harnesses for the use of the army. Some engaged in making cartridge boxes, belts and one establishment making cavalry saddles. In fact, more or less every branch of mechanical were engaged in fitting up army articles. Our little gun factory was pushing on matters in quite a lively way.*
>
> *The hospital was a field for the Ladies to operate, which they did with a good will. They collected large quantities of every description—formed a sewing society for the benefit of the hospital. In a short time large quantities of clothing was made: sheets for bunks, ticks and straw to put in, stoves, kettles, pans, and every thing that should be necessary for hospital purposes*

was procured. Everything was fitted up in a neat and comfortable manner by the ladies and made ready for the reception of sick soldiers.

The Ladies formed a hospital society or Soldiers Relief Society. Mrs. L.H. Carney was elected president of said society and Mrs. Jas. Avent appointed Treasurer. All ever on the go and anxious to see who could render the most aid to the sick, having quite a store room of clothing. As fast as the soldiers would come they were washed and a suit of clean clothes were put on them. A comfortable bunk assigned them, and upon the whole, a hospital did not appear so bad after all.

The meal times were regular and of the best that was to be had. Long table was spread with a clean cloth, plates, knives, and forks and other necessary things to set off, and a plenty to attend the wants of the soldiers. In fact, it was not far behind a second rate Hotel, and all felt a patriotic feeling for the comforts of the soldiers. If there were a chance for a man to get well, he had it here.[1]

The next month, sad news filled the town. A battle had been fought at Mill Springs, also called Fishing Creek, in Kentucky, and Felix Zollicoffer had been killed. Zollicoffer had been a popular Whig leader in Tennessee, serving in the U.S. House of Representatives and then serving as one of the peace commissioners who had tried to avert war in 1860, but he had accepted a commission as a Confederate brigadier. Among those mourning him was Miss Alice Ready, daughter of former congressman Charles Ready Jr. and younger sister of Martha Ready. Writing in her journal on February 11, she noted:

Our feelings, our faith has been tried in another respect, that of giving up our Brothers, friends, all that was dear to us, to this struggle—it may be a sacrifice upon the altar of our Country. Many of the noble and brave have fallen—Mine is too feeble a pen to attempt a eulogy upon them, would that it were in my power to pay a proper respect to the memory of the gallant Zollicoffer—one whom I have known and loved from the earliest days of my childhood—often have I listened to his grave but pleasant discourse at his own hospitable board. We have lost him, a great and good God has seen proper to take him—he was loved and mourned by all—He numbers the third of our generals who have fallen. There are two others, Ballie Peyton and Henry Fogg, both in the early days of their manhood, with a successful career marked out in the future for them, the topmost pinnacle of fame might have been reached by either of them. They to have fallen, gone, but not to

Felix Zollicoffer. *Courtesy of the Tennessee State Library and Archives.*

be forgotten. They will live in the minds of our people as the <u>first</u> Tennessee braves who fell. Though the battle resulted in a defeat for our Southern army, a most ignominious defeat—at Fishing Creek in Kentucky—yet they were brave and did their duty.[2]

Nor was Zollicoffer the only casualty from the area. From the camp of the 20th Tennessee, surgeon Urban G. Owen wrote to his wife:

I am well and hearty. I received a letter from you last Friday week. I looked for one on last Friday but did not get one, but our mails are so uncertain because of high water. I have not heard from Capt. Rucker's Company who was killed, wounded, or taken prisoner. [This unit had fought at Mill Springs.]

I don't know how soon I may be taken prisoner but they will have to outrun little horse before they catch me. But Preachers and Surgeons are never mistreated if they are taken by an Enemy. If our regiment was all taken prisoners I would still do as I do now, doctor them. I would not be tied nor put in close confinement like other officers. And there might be some chance some days for you to see or hear from me, but don't you be uneasy for I will never be taken. Sorry to hear of John Rucker and Bill Hazelwood's death.

The Sun has shone out warm. John has saddled little horse. I will ride this Evening to see our Major who is sick in the country. I want you to write often, once a week or oftener. No more.[3]

FORT DONELSON AND CONFEDERATE RETREAT

Less than a month later, the war came much closer; it came to the front doors of the residents of the county seat of Rutherford County. Ulysses Grant led an amphibious force up the Tennessee River and captured the only effective Confederate defensive work on that stream. Moving overland a few miles, Grant's infantry attacked Fort Donelson, where several dozen Murfreesboro men were serving in the 18th Tennessee under Colonel J.B. Palmer. In three days of fierce fighting, February 14–16, Grant overawed the inept Confederate commanders, and they decided to surrender, all except for Colonel Bedford Forrest, who led several hundred men of his and other commands out of the fort. Now, Nashville was exposed to capture by naval forces, and the main Confederate army at Bowling Green, Kentucky, had no choice but to fall back all the way to Murfreesboro.

John Cedric Spence wrote:

General Johnson had fallen back as far as Murfreesboro with the Confederate troops, after having heavy and fatiguing marches. The soldiers looked jaded and worn out, it having rained quite heavily during their march to this place. They were wet and hungry. But with it all, they

The Storm Breaks in Murfreesboro

put on a cheerful continence. As it was intended to make some stay at this place they set about to pitching tents and put things in order. In a few days they got themselves in a condition to look quite comfortable and satisfied. One morning, early, our ears is greeted by the sound of the horses hoof, the roll of Artillery, wagons, and trains, the heavy tread of the retreating soldier and cavalry in our midst. If dreaming, we are now awakened to a new sense of feeling, that war is spreading its baneful effects through the land and its future effects to be dreaded.[4]

On February 17, the Confederate forces at Nashville were ordered to move to Murfreesboro, the orders authorizing General Crittenden to "press all the wagons you need. Fort Donelson has fallen, and Gen. Floyd's army is captured *after* a gallant defense."[5] Within a few hours, the advance guard of the army reached Murfreesboro and set up camp as Spence described. The pause was temporary because the Confederate High Command viewed the rail junction town of Corinth, Mississippi, as being of greater importance, both for defensive and offensive purposes. From Murfreesboro, the commanding general, Albert Sydney Johnston, reported to Richmond on February 24:

My movements have been delayed by a storm on the 22d washing away pike and railroad bridge at this place. Floyd, 2,500 strong, will march for Chattanooga tomorrow to defend the central line. This army will move on 26th, by Decatur, for the valley of Mississippi; is in good condition and increasing in numbers.[6]

Three days later, on February 27, the orders for the evacuation were issued:

The army will move tomorrow morning at sunrise for Shelbyville. The colonels of all regiments will place all spare wagons at the disposal of the chief quartermaster. The brigadiers and colonels will restrict their officers and men to the smallest possible amount of baggage, and turn over surplus transportation to the chief quartermaster. Maj-Gen. Hardee will assume command of all the cavalry in rear of the army, prescribe the time and manner of their movement, and direct them to destroy all the bridges after they pass over.[7]

Now, only a cavalry screen was left as a rearguard.

The rearguard consisted of about one hundred men under the command of Captain John Hunt Morgan, who was about to make a name for himself

29

as a cavalry raider. Morgan established a camp on the road toward Shelbyville but led a strong picket back to the vicinity of LaVergne so as to keep an eye on any U.S. move from Nashville. There were frequent clashes of patrols as Union troops probed toward Murfreesboro and Morgan tried to keep them back. The U.S. officer in command of these efforts, General Ormsby Mitchell, became rather frustrated with Morgan and the citizens of the area who were so ready to assist Morgan with intelligence, food and shelter.[8]

John Hunt Morgan. *Authors' collection.*

During this stay at Murfreesboro, Mr. Charles Ready visited Morgan's camp and asked the young officer to come to his house for supper. Morgan related, during the meal, that he was a widower and that he was still grieving for his wife, being most of the time "a little sad." To cheer him up, Mr. Ready asked his daughter Mattie to sing for Morgan. Alice Ready recalled her first encounter with the daring, dashing Kentucky cavalryman in her journal entry of March 3, 1862:

> *Morgan is an extremely modest man, but very pleasant and agreeable, though one to see him would scarcely imagine him to be the daring reckless man he is. An immense crowd gathered at the front door to see him, two or three actually came in and stood before the parlor door to see him.*

This visit would become the basis for stories still told in Murfreesboro to this day. John Spence was also impressed with Morgan. He recorded:

> *He is commanding a company of cavalry with some fifty men. He is a man of great energy, and it seems has made his mark where ever he has gone, a Kentuckian by birth. He remained at this place some days after Gen. Johnson left, destroying bridges and tearing up R. Roads which has created a deadly hate by the federal soldiers against him. My son, W.I.S.—impressed with feelings of duty he owed his country,*

volunteered his services as a soldier and joined Morgan in the cavalry service, for weal or woe.[9]

Some of the men from Murfreesboro were not free to fight, fall back or flirt; they were in prisoner of war camps. Narcissa Hall petitioned, unsuccessfully, for the release of her son, who had been captured at Fort Donelson with the rest of Colonel J.B. Palmer's command. Mrs. Hall wrote to Andrew Johnson, the governor appointed by the Lincoln administration:

I have a request to make of you which I hope you may grant. The favor I have to ask is that you will let Alley Abernathy come home on a parole of honor and stay 2 months as a prisoner at home. He is my oldest child I have a living. His brother got killed in blowing rock in a sistern two years ago. My husband died 15 months ago, the only son I have with me had his thigh broke and his breast bone broke and twisted out of its natural place, and is injured inwardly so blood passes from him whenever he fatigues himself, he is disabled for life. It was done by falling from a swing 2 years ago. I have three little girls to raise. If you would grant my request it would confer a great favor on me. You must remember that the privates did not cause this war, they were forced to take up arms on one side or the other and they made their choice to go with the south. As to Alley he said he had rather be in his

Colonel and Mrs. Charles Ready. *Library of Congress (left) and authors' collection.*

grave it was the lords will than to go to war, but he said he would not go as a drafted man.

Mr. Johnson you have power now but recollect the bible says whatsoever measure we mete out it will be measured back again, but I must stop for perhaps I have written more than you will read by remembering the feeling of a parent and grant my request.[10]

It was not until September 1862 that Narcissa saw her wish realized. Her second son was exchanged along with the rest of his regiment at Vicksburg, Mississippi. He was killed in the battle at Murfreesboro in December.

While some families in Murfreesboro waited hopefully for the arrival of U.S. forces so they could openly express their Unionist views, many others waited fearfully. The Ready family was no exception. On Wednesday, March 5, Alice confided to her journal:

Mama has been packing up from them ever since our army left. There is a good deal of fear felt by many persons in regard to their coming. I have not felt the slightest, and do not think I shall when they reach here. My only fear is that they may take Papa prisoner. I think he knows best what to do and am perfectly willing to abide by his decision.[11]

THE YANKEES ARE COMING!

In early March, the last of the Confederates disappeared in the direction of Shelbyville. Before they left, Alice Ready had an encounter with some of the last of the Confederates. She told the story in her journal:

Yesterday the Texas Rangers, which Gen. Hardee had sent back to support Morgan, arrived. When the Army was here, there were several encampments on our farm, everything was being destroyed so rapidly that Papa had a little corn brought to town and put in the ice house. Yesterday Cap, one of the negro men went to the stable to get the horses, when he discovered the soldiers in the ice house after the corn, he came to the house very indignant to tell it. Away I flew up there without hat or bonnet, was out of breath when I reached there, found three or four down in the house, one or two in the garden and numbers of others on the fence. I spoke very politely then—called them gentlemen and asked them not to take the corn. They all left and I came to the house, in about half hour, Albert brought me a note from one of them apologizing for what he had done, signed himself after writing a very nice gentlemanly note C.D. Barnett—Of course I wrote him a note expressing my forgiveness.[12]

Alice would meet the Texas Rangers again in July.

Gray uniforms were replaced by blue a few days later. John Spence told of the event in his diary:

On the tenth of March the ears of the citizens were greeted with the sound of drum and fife, the rattle of artillery, wagons, and columns of marching infantry advancing with glittering bayonets, flags, insignia, and banners flying, prancing steeds, bearing riders with drawn swords, all pomp and display, headed by General Mitchell [sic] in advance.[13]

The general of whom Spence spoke was Ormsby McKnight Mitchel, an astronomer and railroad engineer, who came south with a somewhat jaundiced view of those who supported the Confederacy.[14]

One of the things most of concern to Mitchel was whether or not the citizens had "consented" to the destruction of the road and railroad bridges. This was a curious attitude since it would be standard practice for any army to destroy bridges during a retreat. Having decided that there was some complicity between the citizens and the Confederate army, Mitchel proceeded to act with a heavy hand. John Spence noted:

After General Mitchel got his army pretty well settled, he commences regulating things for the people. He establishes a provost marshal whose duty is to administer oaths and give military passes to citizens. This officer is Oliver Cromwell Rounds.

Among other things the Genl. Undertakes is the repair of the R. Road and Bridges to Nashville, having a great many mechanics in his army and all the necessary tools at hand. He is not long in getting the road in running order. All army stores and provisions up to this time had to be transported by wagon trains from Nashville. Col. John G. Parkhurst was appointed military governor and duly inaugurated and commenced his administration. His territory of government was small but he felt the importance of his position. The reigns began to tighten. The people felt somewhat cramped in their freedom but was [sic] still disposed to feel and act in an independent manner.

The Gen. was not altogether pleased with the inhabitants of this community for the reason they did not shewe a disposition to honor his call nor that friendship was due to him. All this caused the Genl to have very little sympathy for the people and at times they thought he was a little disposed to be a little hard on them.[15]

According to the army regulations of the day, the provost marshal was in charge of seeking out and arresting deserters, spies and civilians suspected of disloyalty. Any theft or misuse of government goods was his responsibility, as was controlling travel within the military zone of occupation. The provost maintained records of who gave paroles and who took the oath of allegiance. Each army post had a provost marshal, and within his jurisdiction, the provost could try cases involving violations of military orders, departures from the laws of war and all other offenses that arose under military jurisdiction. Since Murfreesboro had become a "military zone," the provost was judge and jury, handling many cases that otherwise would have gone before a civilian court.[16] The provost marshal for Murfreesboro was Colonel John G. Parkhurst, commanding the 9th Michigan Infantry; his assistant provost marshal was Captain Oliver Cromwell Rounds of the same regiment. Both these men shared Mitchel's view that harsh treatment was in order for those who continued to be loyal to the Confederacy.

Captain Rounds promulgated an order forbidding anyone in Murfreesboro to engage in business or a profession unless he had taken the oath of allegiance to the United States government. No doctor, lawyer, merchant, undertaker or minister took the oath. Sam Winston, a local businessman and slave trader, was a popular character known throughout the area for his wit and humor. He remarked to a friend, "The time has come when man can't get a lawyer to defend his legal rights; a doctor to protect his health; a druggist to sell him medicines; an undertaker to bury him; nor a preacher to save him from hell."[17]

It was the policy of the Lincoln administration to have civilian government in occupied areas if possible, and an abortive effort to have such was made in Murfreesboro. Mayor John Dromgoole and the board of aldermen had been authorized to serve by Confederate authorities, so General Mitchel called these men in to see if they would take an oath of allegiance to the United States. According to one source, Dromgoole decided to go fishing instead of going to see Mitchel, so he and all the aldermen were removed from office. Taking the place of the old city government were J.M. Thompkins as mayor, R.D. Reed as city recorder and Alford Miller, John Todd, E.S. Jordan, C.B. Huggins and William McKnight as aldermen, while John Jones and V.C. Carter became magistrates and A.B. Gannaway became constable.[18] Military conditions in the town and surrounding area proved to be too fluid for this attempt at Union civilian government to endure, and for most of the war the town was under martial law.

The U.S. soldiers who came to Murfreesboro had varying opinions about the town. One thing caught the eye of them all: the presence of black people. In 1860, about 95 percent of all African Americans lived in the South so that for the men from the North a person of color was something exotic and rare—if, indeed, they had ever seen such a person at all. William Eames, surgeon of an Ohio regiment, wrote to his wife about the town and the camp the army established:

> *The whole journey to this place* [from Nashville] *lies through cotton plantations, and in some fields there are 40 or 50 acres of cotton stubble of last years growth, and on almost every plantation is a building with a cotton press and another with a cotton gin. I inquired of the darkeys on several plantations how much cotton their "massas" raised and they replied some 60 and some as high as 100 bales. I suppose 100 bales would bring 10,000 dollars.*
>
> *It frequently requires 25 or 30 working negroes to take care of the plantations and of course there would be 20 or 30 who would be too old or too young to work and make some 50 to 75 to a plantation.*
>
> *We expect to stay here several days to build the RR bridge over the Stone River which the rebels destroyed. I like the appearance of the village of Murfreesboro very well. The houses are neat and quite large and everything looks comfortable. Our Reg marched through the most important streets to the tunes of "Yankee Doodle" and "Dixie." I saw no Union flags nor any other sign of love for the Union or joy at our arrival.*[19]

John Beatty kept notes about his time in Murfreesboro that were later published as part of his memoir about his military service. For March 30, 1862, he recorded:

> *The colored people of Murfreesboro pour out in great numbers on Sunday evenings to witness dress parade* [the formal military formation], *some of them in excellent holiday attire.*

> *Murfreesboro is an aristocratic town. Many of the citizens have as fine carriages as are to be seen in Cincinnati or Washington. The ladies, so far as I can judge by a glimpse through a carriage window, are richly and elegantly dressed.*
> *The poor whites are as poor as rot, and the rich are very rich. There is no substantial well-to-do middle class. The slaves are, in fact, the middle class here. They are not considered so good, of course, but a great deal better off than the white trash. One enthusiastic colored man said in my hearing this evening: "You look like solgers. No wonder dat you wip de white trash ob de Southern army. Dey ced dey could wip two of you, but I guess one of you could wip two ob dem. You is jes as big as dey is, and maybe a little bigger."*[20]

The daily routing of occupation began to wear on the citizens of Murfreesboro as they came to realize what rights were lost under martial law. Houses were searched for guns, ammunition and any items that might be of military use to Confederates. These searches were quite thorough, involving opening trunks, closets, outbuildings and personal living spaces. Inevitably, such intrusive searches led to pilfering of jewelry, money and other valuables. Any guns, including sporting arms, were seized, and the best of these always seemed to find their way north to some soldier's family. People could be, and were, arrested without charges being brought against them, and they could be held indefinitely at the will of the provost. Passes were required for travel, even within the town limits, so that shopping was impossible without going to the provost and securing such a document. If soldiers on patrol in the country were attacked by Confederate cavalry or by guerrillas, citizens in the vicinity of the attack were arrested and imprisoned, the courthouse being used for this purpose, as was the town jail. If the incarceration was to be lengthy, the persons arrested were sent to Nashville and housed in the state penitentiary. The provost could, and did, seize the property of those living in the vicinity of attacks, with the property being sold and the money sent to the families of those soldiers killed or wounded in the attack.[21]

On April 30, Charles Ready Jr. was one of those arrested. His daughter, Alice, recorded the circumstances in her journal:

> *What a day! I never thought to say that my Father was in the Penitentiary! They grind us closer and closer, until now we scarcely dare to say our house is ours. On 30 minutes warning without allowing him to return even for a change of clothes. Col. Parkhurst, Military Gov, of Murfreesboro wrote*

Papa a note this morning saying it had become necessary for him to take the oath of allegiance to the U.S. Capt Rounds would wait upon him to administer it, which he did. Papa went with him to headquarters, and upon declining to take the proscribed oath—was taken immediately to the depot not allowed to return home—wrote Mama a note for some clothes. Mama cried and screamed—none of the rest of us made the least noise, but what a fountain of pent up feeling there was in our bosom, which pride enabled us to keep her concealed from the detested Federals—and there was a number there. I suppose they intend to do us as much damage as possible—took two of our most valuable negro men out of the field as soon as Papa was arrested. I know not what may be the sentence passed upon our beloved Father, or what may befal our darling Brother—Their fate I know is in the hands of a merciful God. He will not deprive us of all that is dearest. God protect our Father and Brother.[22]

The flow of supplies for men and animals through government channels was never enough to feed all the hungry mouths. The U.S. Army depended on a line of railroad reaching 160 miles via Nashville to Louisville, Kentucky, and the normal accidents of travel were aggravated by the actions of Confederate raiders and guerrillas. Army regulations allowed commanding officers of armies in the field to send out parties to forage; that is, to seize needed foodstuffs from the civilian population. Tragedies resulted from this practice both then and later. In the spring of 1863, foragers from an Ohio regiment came to the farm of Calvin Lowe one day and began systematically to strip the barns, smokehouse and hen roost. Mrs. Minerva Lowe confronted the men and protested their taking all her chickens. In the argument, one of the U.S. soldiers ran his bayonet through Mrs. Lowe's stomach. She was seven months pregnant, and the trauma caused her child to be born prematurely. The child was named Martha but lived only three days, to be followed in death by the mother in less than a month.[23]

William H. King, a boy of fourteen at the time, recalled later that

during the months of May, June, and a part of July, 1862, patrols in squads of 5 to 7 made daily raids through all roads from Murfreesboro, and once or twice a week they would bring wagons for corn. At this time a man named John Halliburton was the manager of the farms of James M. King, Jr., and Charles H. King. They took him and sent him to a northern prison, merely because he was attending to the business of Col. King's two sons. Mr. Halliburton died in prison.[24]

In early May, an incident occurred that brought matters to a crisis point. As Colonel Parkhurst and Captain Rounds were passing along one of the streets in Murfreesboro, a shot was fired. The two men escaped injury, and there is no record of the shot actually being fired at them, nor was any person identified as responsible. However, the matter was reported to Andrew Johnson in Nashville. The governor consulted with E.L. Jordan, G.W. Ashburn and E.D. Wheeler, prominent Unionist citizens of the town. Following this consultation, Johnson wrote to Colonel Parkhurst, "You will at once arrest as many persons as you in your judgment may believe will have a proper effect upon the spirit of insubordination which seems to prevail in that community."[25]

Parkhurst lost no time in arresting twelve leading citizens on no more evidence than their political opinions. The men were W.A. Ransom, Dr. R.S. Wendell, L.M. Maney, J.M. Avent, Jacob Childers, Dr. William S. Blankett, J.M. Dromgoole, Thomas Robertson, Dr. King, G.T. Henderson, F.G. Moseby and J.A. Crockett. The town was subjected to yet more searches, and some two hundred additional guns of various types were confiscated.[26]

The hostages were taken to the state prison in Nashville, and eleven days after Johnson ordered their arrest, they petitioned for release:

The undersigned citizens of Rutherford County Tennessee, having been arrested by the Military authorities of the United States, and being now held as hostages, to secure the safety of Murfreesboro, and as a measure to guard against the repetition of unlawful acts, said to have been committed, by residents of our town, against officers and soldiers of the Federal army stationed at Murfreesboro, and desiring to return home to our families, do hereby pledge our honor, to demean ourselves as peaceable and orderly citizens by yielding obedience to the Constitution and laws of the United States. We will give no aid to, nor sympathize with men who would attempt to waylay and shoot others, but will use best efforts to discover such offenders, be they friend or foes, and bring them to just punishment. We also express our disapproval of irregular warfare, carried on in the country by lawless bands, detrimental to the interests of the country, peculiarly annoying to the people and very destructive to life and property. We further pledge ourselves to use our exertions in favor of these our sentiments, among our fellow citizens, and by the best means in our power, to obtain the co-operation of our countrymen in the suppression of wrongs by individuals or by bands of disorderly men against the Federal Army, its officers or any portion of our citizens.[27]

Release came a few days later following the posting of bonds of $10,000 each.

The Storm Breaks in Murfreesboro

Demonstrations of sentiment, large and small, kept the town on edge. Kate Carney recorded one such event:

> *I forgot to mention in here about a grand parade they had one day over a little secession flag they got from some private family. Pretended as if they had gotten it in a fight and tied it to the mane of one of their horses and dragged the flag and strewed flowers where the flag went along. That was a contemptible act, equaled only by the arrest of Mr. Winship, to make him look at their Union flag that Mrs. Matilda Spence and her niece Mary made them, just because he helped raise the Confederate flag when it was first hoisted in our town, but he would not look up, but smoked away like he didn't care a fig for all of them and their old flags.*[28]

Mr. Winship, a leading secessionist, was arrested solely for the purpose of humiliating him by forcing him to go the courthouse to witness the daily raising of the U.S. flag by the military garrison there.

Local Confederate supporters replied in kind. The *Nashville Daily Union* reported that on July 4 several families flying the U.S. flag were the targets of rock throwing on the part of roving bands of children. It was the view of the paper that while the actions of the children were bad, they were not as bad as the attitude of the parents who knew of and encouraged such things.[29]

The clouds of war had rolled over Murfreesboro, and the air was charged with emotions. Then, out of this electrical atmosphere came a lightning bolt.

3

A Bold Flash of Lightning

A LIGHTNING RAID

Life seemed good to Colonel Henry C. Lester of the 3rd Minnesota, commanding all U.S. troops in the immediate vicinity of Murfreesboro. He had a position well behind the front lines, there was plenty of food and the weather was hot but dry. His only problem was that some of the units in his command argued with one another a lot, something not uncommon when units were composed of men from the same state, and rivalry easily flared when state pride was invoked. In an attempt to maintain good order and discipline, he placed most of the 9th Michigan Infantry on the east side of town on the edge of the lawn of Oaklands, the estate of the Maney family. There was a large spring there, and the infantry's position blocked the main access road from the east, the Liberty Pike. Five companies, half of this regiment, had been detached to Tullahoma, Tennessee, leaving four to camp at Oaklands and one company to bivouac at the courthouse to act as a provost guard. Just a few hundred yards beyond the camp of the 9th Michigan was the position of some eighty men of the 7th Pennsylvania Cavalry, the main mounted force, which provided scouting and pickets on the roads leading into town from all directions.

To make life easier for this limited number of horse-soldiers, Colonel Lester brought all patrols back to town in the early evening so the men and animals could rest in camp. The picket posts were manned twenty-four hours daily. The 3rd Minnesota Infantry and four guns of the 1st Kentucky

Battery were camped on a ridge north of town, about one and a quarter miles from the Michigan encampment.

The only enemy in the vicinity, Lester was confident, was a small cavalry raiding party under John Hunt Morgan, which he believed had passed well above Murfreesboro and was on its way to Kentucky. The main Confederate force was somewhere near Chattanooga, although there were scattered guerrillas in the cedar thickets of Middle Tennessee. These made it necessary to send out guard details for foragers and even to protect Unionist citizens.[1]

The good times for Colonel Lester came to an abrupt end on July 12, when a train pulled into the station bearing Brigadier General Thomas T. Crittenden and Colonel W.W. Duffield. Crittenden took over command of the garrison, while Duffield was to command the 9th Michigan. Crittenden did not approve of the scattered nature of the camps and immediately began looking for a central place to concentrate his troops. Further, he was displeased with the practice of pulling in the cavalry patrols at night but decided to wait a day or so to change the practice. After spending a busy day shaking up the routine of the town, Crittenden reviewed the death sentences that had been reached by a court-martial the day before. Six civilians had been condemned to hang, two of them having been ruled to be spies and the other four in retaliation for attacks on U.S. soldiers. These sentences were confirmed and a minister sent for to spend the night with the condemned men. Their quarters in the town jail were cramped since 150 civilians from Murfreesboro and the surrounding country were confined there.

Captain Oliver Cromwell Rounds, of the 9th Michigan, was not at all tolerant of the Rebel sympathies of the people of the area. He had come south to crush the rebellion, and he was in a fair way of living up to his namesake, the grim old Puritan of seventeenth-century England. The earliest history of the events about to unfold noted of Rounds:

The Federals exercised a harsh and arrogant dominion over the people of Murfreesboro and the surrounding country who had been made the victims of constant and wrongful oppressive exaction and restrictions discreditable to the age or civilized warfare. The provost-marshal, churlish when not cruel, it would seem, delighted in harassing the women.

Apparently, Rounds was not "churlish" to all the ladies; he was engaged to marry Corine Reeves, a local girl, on the night of July 13. Corine was seventeen years old and was probably an orphan who was living with her grandmother.[2]

General Thomas T. Crittenden. *Library of Congress.*

The general's rest—and that of all residents, both civilian and military—was undisturbed until day began to break, even though the lightning had been drawing near all night.

Bedford Forrest had established a reputation as a daring leader by February 1862. Promoted to brigadier, he had been sent to blunt the U.S. advance on Chattanooga. By July 8, he had his men ready to ride and began his bold move on Murfreesboro with its complacent U.S. garrison. Forrest would take with him the 8ᵗʰ Texas Cavalry, commonly called Terry's Texas Rangers, under Colonel John Wharton; the 2ⁿᵈ

General Nathan Bedford Forrest. *Library of Congress.*

Georgia Cavalry under Colonel J.K. Lawton; the 1ˢᵗ Georgia Regiment under Colonel James J. Morrison (only a small part of this unit had received weapons, so only a battalion-sized force was on the expedition); a part of the 1ˢᵗ Kentucky Cavalry under Colonel Adam Johnson; and a battalion of Tennessee troopers commanded by Baxter Smith.[3]

The column that rode out of the Sequatchie Valley on July 8 included only able-bodied fighting men. All cooks, body servants and men with weak horses had been left behind. Hard riding brought the 1,500 men to Altamont at the top of the Cumberland Plateau on July 10, and a day was spent resting and taking care of final details. On the twelfth, the men rode down the western face of the plateau into McMinnville and on to Woodbury, reaching there about 11:00 p.m. The noise of the horses soon awakened the entire village, and food was soon making its welcome appearance in the hungry, tired ranks. Also sweeping along the line was the news that most of the men of the place had been arrested that day and led off to Murfreesboro to be held as hostages. The food and the motivation helped keep the men in rank for the rest of the night. There was a hint of gray in the east when the column halted on the Liberty Pike outside Murfreesboro. Silently, the 8ᵗʰ Texas sent forward a picked unit to capture the U.S. picket post. This vital task was led by Captain Fred James, an infantry officer whose home was Murfreesboro. James was on leave in Chattanooga when he somehow heard about Forrest's plans, and he volunteered to accompany the raid. James would fight another day at Murfreesboro; he was killed in sight of his own home on December 31, 1862.[4]

James returned with fifteen prisoners, no shots having been fired. Colonel Wharton immediately ordered his bugler to sound the charge, and Texas Rangers, Georgia Cracker Cavaliers and Kentucky and Tennessee boys pounded down the streets of Murfreesboro. The camp of the 7th Pennsylvania Cavalry was overrun, and shouting, shooting Rebs swarmed among the tents of the 9th Michigan, scattering buckshot and pistol balls on all sides. One of the attackers was Private E.H. Ross, of Company A, and he would not live to see the end of the day. He had written what proved to be his last letter home just before setting out on the raid. In the letter, he said, "Tell father and mother not to forget me."[5]

As the 8th Texas turned into the grounds of Oaklands, the 2nd Georgia raced for the courthouse square to subdue the provost guard, capture the high-ranking officers known to be quartered in the hotel and private homes on the square and release the prisoners in the jail. One man who helped with this task really "had no dog in the fight"; Pat Carney had just arrived from Ireland, exiled because of his opposition to British rule. A local author said:

> *Pat was aroused from sleep, it being about four o'clock of a Sunday morning, and instantly sprang from his bed, though not knowing what the excitement was about, seized his old trusty musket, rushed out and joined the Confederate forces and made a full hand at fighting during the battle. He then joined Forrest's troops on the return to McMinnville and remained with the command until the surrender.*[6]

The 1st Georgia, along with the Kentucky and Tennessee detachments, would ride for the camp of the 3rd Minnesota and the 1st Kentucky Artillery. Theirs was the largest body of foes, and theirs would be the longest fight.

Recovering from their initial shock and surprise, the four companies of the 9th Michigan rallied and fortified their camp with overturned wagons, bales of hay and sacks of corn. They then repelled several mounted attacks, despite the wounding of Colonel Duffield and his replacement by Lieutenant Colonel James Parkhurst. Duffield was carried into the Maney house and recuperated with the family for many weeks. During his convalescence, his wife came from Detroit to be his nurse, and she, too, stayed in the Maney house. In 1866, Duffield sent the Maneys a silver service.[7]

Courthouse. *Courtesy of Bill Jakes.*

At the town square, the fighting was equally fierce. The provost guards and officers who were in private houses and the hotel were quickly "gobbled up," with many of them being captured in their nightclothes. It was rumored that Captain Rounds was found in the bed of his fiancée, nestled between two feather mattresses with the bed fully made up with quilts and pillows and his wife-to-be attempting to stand guard at the door.[8]

General Crittenden was captured in the hotel where he was staying. The proprietor of the hotel was Mrs. Hagan, and when the general saw the town square full of Confederates, he handed his pistol and sword to her and asked her to negotiate a surrender for him.[9] He was a prisoner of war from July to October and was exonerated by a court-martial following his release, but the utter success of Forrest's raid at Murfreesboro spelled the end of his military career, and he resigned from the army in May 1863.

Companies E and F of the 2nd Georgia were assigned the task of capturing the courthouse and its garrison. Four men volunteered to batter down the door with an axe. Two of this party, Gus Darden and James Hicks, were killed. Henry Clay Burr got into the courthouse and collected furniture from the offices to start a fire on the brick floor of the building, literally "smoking out" the Yankees on the upper floors.[10]

A Bold Flash of Lightning

Across the street at the jail, an atrocity was being narrowly prevented. When the guards at the jail, members of the 9th Michigan Infantry, realized that the prisoners were about to be rescued, they attempted to murder the men confined in the cells. First they fired into the cells, but the men inside pressed against the front walls and stayed out of the line of fire. Then an attempt was made to burn all 150 men alive. Captain William Richardson was one of the men in the cells. In later years, he was an attorney in Huntsville, Alabama, and he recounted the events for John Allan Wyeth:

Just about daylight on the morning of the 13th I was aroused from sleep by my companion, Paul, who had caught me by the arm and was shaking me, saying, "Listen, listen!" I started up, hearing a strange noise like the roar of an approaching storm. We both leaped to our feet and stood upon an empty box which had been given us in lieu of a chair, and looked out through the small grating of our prison window. The roar grew louder and came nearer, and in a very few seconds we were sure we could discern the clatter of horses' feet upon the hard turnpike. In a moment more there could be no doubt as to the riders of these horses, for on the morning air there came to our ears with heartfelt welcome the famous rebel yell, the battle-cry of the Confederate soldiers.

Within the prison yard one company of Federal troops had been stationed, and, seeing they were about to be surrounded by the Confederates and that our rescue was sure, several of these soldiers in a wicked mood rushed into the passageway in front of our cell and attempted to shoot us before they ran from the building. We only saved ourselves by running forward and crouching in the corner of the cell by the door. Before leaving the jail one of the Federal guards struck a match, and, lighting a bundle of papers, shoved this beneath the flooring of the hall-way where the planks were loose, and, to our horror we realized he was determined to burn us to death before the rescue party could break open the door. When the Southern riders reached us the fire was already under good headway, and the jailer had fled with the keys. It seemed as if we still were doomed. The metal doors were heavy, and it was not until some of our men came in with a heavy iron bar that the grating was bent back sufficiently at the lower corner to permit us to be dragged through as we lay flat upon the floor.[11] *Questioned later in the day about his treatment, Richarson pointed out the man who had tried to burn the prisoners alive. His name does not appear on the list of prisoners paroled.*

One of the defenders of the courthouse was Robert Henry Hendershott, twelve years old. Seeing an officer approach, the boy soldier took careful aim and shot the man out of his saddle. The officer was Colonel Richard Sanders, sixty years old and accompanying the raid as a volunteer. Sanders rode out of town on Church Street to the home of William Ledbetter, where he was offered shelter. The next day, U.S. troops came to the house and surrendered to the helpless officer just so they could get parole to go home. Hendershott remained in the army until the 1880s.[12]

Forrest led the men from the courthouse area to the camp of the 3rd Minnesota once the fighting downtown was over. The Minnesota regiment was in a strong position, so Forrest used his usual tactic of outflanking its line and hitting its camp from the rear. This move pinned the Minnesotans in place but did not bring about their surrender. So Forrest left a holding force to "keep the skeer on 'em" and led the rest of his men to the Maney house to confront the 9th Michigan. The Texas Rangers had rested and re-formed, so the appearance of Forrest with reinforcements was very discouraging to Lieutenant Colonel Parkhurst. After a consultation with the wounded Colonel Duffield, a decision was made to accept the demand to surrender that Forrest had presented. Parkhurst would later return to Murfreesboro and marry Josephine Reeves, younger sister of Corine.

Forrest then rode back to the 3rd Minnesota and told the Minnesotans what had just happened. Colonel Lester asked to speak to Duffield. Forrest readily consented and, in escorting the colonel to and from the Maney house, played another of his patented tricks. Forrest moved his men from place to place so Lester counted them over and over. Returning to his men totally overawed, Lester ordered a surrender, despite the objections of many of his men who felt they could keep up a successful defense.

By late afternoon, the fighting was over, and the weary but happy Rebs began to collect their booty and make a list of their prisoners. The officers of both sides gathered at Oaklands and shared a meal of sweet potatoes and black-eyed peas. By nightfall, all the Southern boys, except those too badly wounded to be moved, were gone. The next day, at McMinnville, all the U.S. enlisted men were paroled and allowed to go home, while the officers began their journey to prison camps.

The indefatigable diarist John Spence noted that twenty-one U.S. soldiers were killed at Oaklands, along with two African Americans who had been employed as servants in the camp; there were no Confederate dead at that location. In the fighting at the courthouse, twenty-three Confederates were killed, but there were no U.S. dead there. In the attack on the Minnesota position, two were killed on each side. One citizen, Mr. Nesbit, was killed, and a Mr. Booker was seriously wounded. One curious fact is contained in the report of Lieutenant Colonel Parkhurst, of the 9th Michigan. He stated in his official report that "there were also a large number of Negroes attached to the Texas and Georgia troops who were armed, equipped, and took part in the several engagements with my forces during the day."[13] Forrest had ordered that all cooks, body servants and grooms be left at Chattanooga, so none of this category of men was present. Just what did Lieutenant Colonel Parkhurst see?

AFTER THE STORM

Deep down, the Confederate sympathizers knew their moment of glory would be short-lived, but they were determined to enjoy it to the fullest. At least two of them wrote accounts of the day in their journals. One of these writers was Sally Iven, a fourteen-year-old girl who lived on the main street leading to the courthouse square. Sally wrote:

> *Yesterday was a Sunday never to be forgotten by the people of Murfreesboro. At daylight we were aroused by terrific yelling and the firing of guns at Maney's Grove where the 9th Michigan Regiment was camped. Before we could collect our senses the cook came running crying, "Marse John, de town is full of Rebels!" We ran to the door just out of bed and, sure enough, there were our boys in gray dashing across the street going to the courthouse where the Provost Guard were quartered and soon the streets were swarming with them.*
>
> *Forrest and his men made a forced march from McMinnville Saturday night and dashed in on the Yankees taking them wholly by surprise. They rushed in wild confusion from their lines undressed seeking shelter from the Terrible Rebs. They were soon captured.*
>
> *Forrest then hastened to the assistance of those who were besieging the courthouse. Soon nothing could be heard but the clash of arms, the cracking of guns and the shouts of our soldiers. Papa was out gathering in the wounded and dead. Our house was soon full. The downstairs floor of wounded while the floor of his furniture house was covered with the dead.* [In nineteenth-century usage, "furniture" referred to harness for horse, so the dead were placed in a room off the barn.] *When the dead were moved a flattened ball fell from the head of*

our of our soldiers. Papa gave it to me. I will keep it. [A note written in the margin says: "I have it still. March 15, 1907.] *While Papa was busy on the streets Mama and I were busy with the wounded and feeding all who passed. On Saturday Ma had light bread and boiled ham prepared for Sunday. She soon had this sliced and in a basket with a large bucket of buttermilk with a cup for them to drink from and the cook assembled a large bucket of wheat coffee. I stood on the pavement and as the soldiers passed they were invited to "Take a drink and a bite" as long as the refreshments lasted.*

While standing there I realized something of what the soldier feels in battle for scattering Yankees were firing at us from vacant houses and balls were whizzing by our heads and yet I felt no fear but stood my ground until the Rebels made off.

By 7 O'clock the town was ours and meantime all things were made secure here. Forrest dashed on the Stone River where the 3ʳᵈ Minnesota Regiment was camping. Here the Yankees had the advantage also for they had four pieces of artillery while we had none. At ten O'clock the cannonading which had been kept up all morning began to get nearer until shells were falling in town. Several fell or burst in front of our house but the brave boys in gray finally won the day and were in entire possession of everything, but before morning they had taken their prisoners who were able to travel and gone back to McMinnville.

Last night I sat up with a wounded Rebel, Mr. Hamil from Georgia, who was thought to be mortally wounded. While Papa and some other citizens were out burying the dead, they dug trenches and put all the Rebels to themselves and all the Yankees to themselves. This morning ambulances came round and gathered up the few remaining wounded who could possibly be moved for we are expecting the Yankees from Nashville any time. Mr. Hamil went. He would not consent to being left behind.

It is so delightful to our feelings and restful to the eye to be able to look out and see not a blue coat anywhere.[14]

Another diarist was Kate Carney. She was older than Sally Iven and was not bold enough to venture into the street; nevertheless, she saw a good deal of what happened and wrote about it immediately:

July 13 How to begin I know not. It has surely been an eventful day. I was aroused early this morning by firing. I knew the firing must come from our own brave boys. Spring from my bed, rush to the window, called to cousin Ann & Bettie, we dressed hurriedly, not knowing what moment our house & yard would be full to overflowing with either our men or the frightened Yankees. The blue coats began to make a bee line through our yard and front yard, asking Pa to protect them, but he told them to push on, and acting on his advice they kept moving. Just think, only the day before they were our masers, I thought what would be our fate, if our poor fellows were whipped. The engagement grew general in a few moments. Persons dared not venture out on the square, were afraid to venture up town, as they were firing from the houses, so much it was dangerous to go on the street and if they did a report & a vacant saddle would be seen as the horse would dash by, carrying their fate to their comrades. Our boys, after forming behind some one story buildings, made a bold rush gaining the court house, but many fell ere they reached the door, and although the Yankees had every advantage they were forced to surrender, & our prisoners turned out to seek their families & friends.

In the meanwhile they had attacked the camp down by the river where the battery was stationed, & on the approach of our men threw themselves into a hollow square with their artillery, pointed to resist a determined attack, and as our men had nothing but shot guns they could not get in range & were compelled to fall back three times. But later in the day a flag of truce was sent & in a few minutes they consulted and surrendered. Without a single piece of artillery besides being the attacking party I am sure the hand of Providence guided and directed our boys, for without a higher power that handful of men could never have succeeded against such odds. Our Great Father saw our sufferings and travails.[15]

Not all those present in Murfreesboro shared the feelings of elation evidenced by the two lady diarists. Surgeon William Eames, who had come to town with an Ohio regiment in the spring, was caught up in the fighting as wounded poured into the hospital he served. The U.S. Army had taken over the hospital first established by the Confederates in the buildings of Union College. The hospital was on the road the Georgia troopers followed as they charged into town to attack the courthouse, so Eames had been awakened by their passing. In writing to his wife to tell her that he was safe, the good doctor admitted that he had been quite sick for several days and was unable even to sit up but that the passage of the Rebs had miraculously cured him so that he was out of bed and dressed in only a few minutes. Confident in a U.S. victory, he was much chagrined to find himself temporarily a prisoner of war until the Confederate withdrawal, at which time he was left at the hospital.[16]

Colonel Henry C. Lester, of the 3rd Minnesota, would be the object of scorn and ridicule on the part of his comrades in arms for the rest of his life. In a paper delivered to a veterans' reunion more that twenty-five years after the end of the war, Dr. Albert C. Wedge, one of the men who had served as a surgeon in the 3rd, ended his account of the fight the regiment made before its surrender by saying:

> *It is my unpleasant duty to again refer to Col. Lester. I must state that the disaster of July 13th 1862 was the result of incompetence and cowardice of Col. Henry C. Lester. How he came to be such a disappointment is a mystery…He disgraced himself and humiliated all the officers and men of his command. He and the few officers who favored surrender were dismissed promptly from the service.*[17]

The African American population showed the effect of the raid as well. The policy of the United States was not yet one of abolition, at least not officially. Many of the men in the army saw ending slavery as an effective method of weakening the Confederacy and, thus, speeding up the end of the war. On the higher political levels, there was concern that ending slavery would alienate many of the pro-Union, old Whig slave owners whom Lincoln hoped to recruit into the Republican Party. In 1862, it was not uncommon for those slaves who came into the lines of the U.S. Army to be sent back to their masters. Still, the African American community knew that a U.S. victory would mean a major change in their status, and signs of support for the Union cause had not been lacking. The success of Forrest's raid put a damper on such expressions. Although the presence of the Confederates was brief, it was obvious that they could return at any time in even larger numbers. Until it was clear who might be the ultimate victor, the course of wisdom was to stay as neutral as possible in action and open expression. So, while the boys in blue might be welcomed, the African American workers went back into the fields and kitchens and carried on as before.

The guerrillas who had been lurking in the cedar thickets around Murfreesboro took advantage of the absence of troops of either army to raid the town. On July 16, the firm of Hornbeck & Forsyth reported that about twenty-five guerrillas commanded by one calling himself Captain Bond came to Hornbeck's residence and forced him to go open the store.

There, they took about $200 in goods and a horse worth $200. Some of the "better citizens" of Murfreesboro attempted to talk the guerrillas out of robbing the store, but to no effect. Hornbeck, who had Union sympathies, was taken to a wounded lieutenant left behind by the raiders, and Hornbeck gave a written parole not to fight against the Confederacy. In conversation with citizens, the Bond company men said they had shot several U.S. pickets on the Lebanon Pike near Pierce's Mill.[18]

Nashville got a firsthand account of the affair at Murfreesboro a few days later as the U.S. soldiers paroled by Forrest at McMinnville began to reach that town. Elizabeth Harding, a member of a wealthy pro-Confederate family, wrote to a friend, "The Yankees captured by Forrest at Murfreesboro speak of him in the highest terms—he took them on one day's march toward McMinnville before he paroled them. They were allowed to ride when tired and the last crust was divided with them."[19]

The return of the U.S. Army to Murfreesboro was only a question of time. On July 20, Kate Carney recorded in her diary:

This morning the first thing I heard was many voices at once, & in finding out who they were, learned it was 9 Yankees that had come & ordered their breakfast. Only 7 remained, the other two thought it would be too long preparing, said if we didn't give them something to eat they would take every horse on the place. Pa was the only member of the family that went in where they were. They ate everything up, and the cook had to get a fresh supply. Scarcely had they gone when two more scamps said they had orders to take every horse they saw. Pa & Ma went out and talked quite plain to them, said they should not have them until a written order was shown. One of them told Ma if she were a man he would whip her.

The Carneys fed soldiers all day in groups of four and five and eventually asked for a guard to be sent to their house. An officer came and spent the night, but Kate did not go in to supper because "I dislike very much to eat at the table with the Yankees."[20]

As was usually the case in a battle, it was the doctors who got the last word. The final report concerning the effects of Forrest's Birthday Raid on Murfreesboro appear in a letter Dr. William Eames wrote to his wife on August 9:

We have now 160 patients and probably shall get 20 more to-day. We took in 45 yesterday & some of them were very sick…Some of the gun-shot wounds are very bad yet tho I think that none will die. There is one who was shot in the back of the neck & the ball lodged in the spinal canal. He is completely paralyzed on one side but now sits up part of the time (8 or 10 hours per day) says he feels "bully." Others have bones broken & terrible discharges of pus but are doing admirably I think. We had 77 gun shot wounds in July and lost only 2. There were 12 cases of fracture, 42 of Typhoid Fever, etc.[21]

The letter is a good reminder that infection was a problem Civil War medicine was not able to handle and that disease was a greater danger than combat. The record of recovery, two deaths out of seventy-seven wounds, is excellent. The last of the wounded from the bold flash of lightning would not leave town for many months.

Politically and militarily, skies had not cleared over Murfreesboro. A bold flash of lightning and a brief storm had produced momentary change, but greater storms and dramatic changes were soon to come.

4

A Southern Wind Before Winter

THE WIND SHIFTS

As more boys in blue moved into Murfreesboro to replace those Forrest had captured, they could not know the raid was a prelude of things to come. Strategically, a Southern wind would begin to blow and would last until winter arrived. The days of the renewed occupation were numbered. On July 17, 1862, John Spence noted in his journal:

> *We are greeted with an advance-guard of the union army, making their appearance for the purpose of reoccupying the town. Shortly after, they came with greater force.*
> *The Union men took charge of their own men and permitted the citizens to continue the nursing of the wounded confederate soldiers. As fast as either was sufficiently recovered, they were sent off to their proper destination.*[1]

Kate Carney also commented on the return of the U.S. Army. She noted that on July 17, only a few men entered the town, and they came under a flag of truce to inquire about the wounded. The next day, the main force arrived in the early afternoon—Kate said "about dinnertime," which would have been 1:00 p.m.—and stopped all travel, even along the city streets. Soon, houses were being searched and civilians arrested. Fearing that her house was to be searched, Kate hid the Confederate flag she had sewn "in my bosom." By the nineteenth, an order had been issued that all government items taken from the various army camps were to be turned in; these proved to be clothes, most of which had been picked up by African Americans. One of the paroled Yankees brought the Reeves family a letter from Captain O.C. Rounds, but he never returned himself.[2]

The commander of the occupying troops was General William Nelson, called "Bull" because of both his size and his temper. A naval officer of more than twenty years' service, Nelson had led the effort to raise troops in his home state of Indiana and had been offered a commission in the army as a result. His behavior toward civilians, especially women, was offensive to many Southerners. In Murfreesboro, Nelson insisted that the proprietor of his boardinghouse turn out all her other boarders so she could give him her full attention. On one occasion, Nelson threatened his hostess with arrest because his breakfast biscuits were too hard.[3] A few weeks later, he would be shot dead by a fellow officer who was not prosecuted for the matter. One of the first acts of General Nelson was to order all pro-Confederate slave owners to send in a fixed number of their slaves to be used as laborers, building fortifications for the protection of the town against future attack.

Among those who resisted the order were James King Moore and his relative William King. As a result, both men became targets for extensive foraging. In the month of August 1862, General Nelson sent 140 to 150 wagons to the plantation of William King and seized 3,500 bushels of corn, as well as numerous other items such as poultry and meat.[4]

Searches of houses extended from the town into the surrounding countryside and were carried out in a way intended to intimidate the civilian population, as well as to apprehend any Confederates who had infiltrated the area. William King described the process in a memoir written after the war:

> These searches were often made in the still, dead hours of the night, after suddenly awakening us, demanding entrance without telling us who they were or what they wanted...One night these marauders came frightening us to an alarming degree. We had all the outer doors barred and the window shutters fastened. Mother pleadingly asked them who they were and what they wanted. The only answer was "We want to come in the house." She refused to unbar the doors. Simultaneously some of them roughly thrust their fists through the side-lights along the back hall door, reached around and unbarred the door.

A Southern Wind Before Winter

Then the Yankees deluged the hall, while others prized open the window-blinds on the rear of the house, opening into old Grandmother's room. Those who entered the hall walked to the front door where Mother and I were standing, unbarred and opened the door. The officer in command came in saying, "I want to search the house for Captain Lytle and John King." Mother said, "Why did you not tell me that instead of frightening me as you have done?"...Although they seemed so sanguine in their expectations, and proceeded to search every nook and corner of the house, they failed to find the one they sought.[5]

Miles away from Murfreesboro, strategic decisions were being made that would affect dramatically the civilian inhabitants and the military garrison. The U.S. Army under General Henry Halleck had occupied Corinth, Mississippi, with the Confederates falling back to Tupelo, where a new commander was named: General Braxton Bragg. Soon, Bragg made one of his best decisions of the war, while Halleck made one of his worst.

Instead of pressing on with his superior numbers to take Vicksburg, Halleck broke up his force into small units and stood still. In north Alabama, General Don Carlos Buell was ordered to push east toward Chattanooga, with his supplies coming along the Memphis & Charleston Railroad (M&C) from Memphis via Corinth. An additional line of supply was to be the Louisville & Nashville Railroad (L&N), thence from Nashville southeast along the Nashville & Chattanooga Railroad (N&C). Bragg took advantage of Halleck's pause to shift his army by rail from Tupelo to Chattanooga and to begin a move into Kentucky.

The raid Forrest made on Murfreesboro revealed how vulnerable Buell's line of supply was. Soon after the Birthday Raid, General Frank Armstrong would lead Confederate cavalry into west Tennessee to attack the M&C, while Forrest and Morgan would operate against the L&N and the N&C. The movement of Bragg from Chattanooga north and west into Kentucky, in conjunction with the cavalry attacks, forced Buell to retire from Alabama and Tennessee. Except for garrisons at Corinth, Mississippi; Memphis; and Nashville, a Southern wind blew strong.

In late August, about a month after the reoccupation, the U.S. Army began to leave Murfreesboro. John Spence wrote of the event in his diary. On August 20,

the main body was passing Murfreesboro, continuing for several days. Retreating men shew [sic] a disposition to be destructive. While passing here, several attempts were made to fire the town. A fire was started in the court house on the stairway, and by mere accident was extinguished—another in the Telegraph Printing office. This was stopped in time without any injury.

There were many family residences on the road to Nashville that was [sic] burned down by the retreating soldiers. A great deal of this firing was done for the purpose of robbery and some for the purpose of gratifying a low, malicious feeling, as they had come more to destroy than to restore the country to peace.[6]

One of those who experienced vandalism at the hands of Buell's soldiers was Charles W. Anderson, whose home was just outside Murfreesboro. Anderson was a vice-president of the N&C and had been active in assisting sick and wounded Confederates. On the day McCook's Division passed his house, Anderson and his wife were not at home, having gone to visit a sick neighbor. The U.S. soldiers went into Anderson's house and looted the premises, even taking outside the portraits of his parents. Since no one wanted the pictures, the frames were smashed and the canvas slashed with sabers. The house, outbuildings and even the houses occupied by the African American slaves were burned.[7]

On September 5, the rear guard of Buell's force left Murfreesboro as Forrest and Morgan harassed the retreating U.S. forces. Morgan was something of the darling of the hour since he had led his men back into the area early in the summer and had penetrated into Kentucky on at least two occasions. He had set up a headquarters at Sparta, Tennessee, east of Murfreesboro, and had been a constant thorn in the Yankees' flesh ever since, with successful raids on Gallatin (where, in August, he destroyed twin tunnels on the L&N, taking the line out of service for several months) and victories in numerous skirmishes between Nashville and Murfreesboro. Forrest arrived in the area about October 1 to supplement Morgan's efforts and to organize fresh troops, drawing on the ranks of the Tennessee militia, as well as on new recruits. Although there were not many Confederates in the town, there were no Yankees. The main Southern army, under Braxton Bragg, was maneuvering in Kentucky, and only slowly did forces accumulate in Middle Tennessee.

The Battle of Perryville was fought in Kentucky on October 8, 1862, and resulted in the retreat of the Confederates from the Bluegrass State. Falling back through the Cumberland Gap to Knoxville, moving on to Chattanooga and then northwest to Murfreesboro, the army spread itself in a position to block the numerous roads leading out of Nashville from east to south to west. The cavalry screen stretched even beyond the infantry lines in an attempt to protect an area rich in food, as well as supplying the horses and mules on which the transportation of the army depended. Murfreesboro became a bustling army headquarters.

All was not well in the ranks of the Southern forces. Many generals, and a number of enlisted men, felt Bragg had bungled the Kentucky Campaign. The army had stood across Buell's line of retreat at one point but had stepped aside, allowing the U.S. forces to reach Louisville. Then Bragg had allowed himself to be taken by surprise when the enemy advanced against

Braxton Bragg. *Library of Congress.*

him so that the Confederate forces were scattered and in no position to fight a successful battle at Perryville. In an attempt to calm the troubled waters, Murfreesboro made ready to receive a distinguished visitor.

A PRESIDENTIAL VISIT

Jefferson Davis knew his visit to Murfreesboro was necessary, but he wished it were not. The military situation in the western theater, Mississippi and Tennessee, demanded immediate attention. Bragg's innovative use of rail transportation had led to the Kentucky Campaign, which allowed the South to reverse much of the Northern gains of the early part of the year, but that relief was now ebbing. Grant was moving out of Memphis, heading for Vicksburg via Holly Springs and Oxford, while William S. Rosecrans, who had replaced Don Carlos Buell, was back in Nashville. In addition to quieting the criticism of Bragg, some long-term strategy was needed for the western area.

Jefferson Davis. *Library of Congress.*

President Davis first met with department commander General Joseph E. Johnston to pressure the general to send infantry to Mississippi to oppose Grant's move. Johnston was worried that if infantry were sent from Bragg, then Tennessee would be lost. Johnston favored using the cavalry in both Tennessee and Mississippi to raid Union supply lines to hamper their advance. After meeting Johnston in Chattanooga, and agreeing in principle to the use of cavalry, Davis moved on to Murfreesboro.

General George Washington Custis Lee, the son of Robert E. Lee, accompanied Davis as his aide, so the public had a double reason to be curious about and welcoming of the visit. Both Lee and Davis were to be guests at Oaklands, the home of Dr. and Mrs. Lewis Maney. The house was full of Maney family and relations, but the distinguished visitors were given large rooms at the front of a new wing of the house. Hospitality was abundant, even though the war had begun to produce shortages in such items as sugar and coffee. Flour, rice, meat and other commodities were still plentiful, and the prices were still reasonable. Davis and Lee would be made comfortable and entertained in a lavish manner.

Braxton Bragg set a happy mood for the visit by issuing General Order #155 congratulating John Hunt Morgan for his December 7 attack on Hartsville, Tennessee, and the capture of 1,800 prisoners of war. Bragg

The Davis Room. *Courtesy of Oaklands.*

noted, "The intelligence, zeal, and gallantry displayed by them will serve as an example and an incentive to still more honorable deeds. Each corps engaged in the action will in future bear on its colors the name of the memorable field."[8]

President Davis needed a good night's sleep at Oaklands because Saturday would be a very busy day. The first order of business was a meeting with General Bragg in which Davis wanted to drive home the point that more troops should be sent to Mississippi to defend that state; specifically, Davis wanted to send the eight-thousand-man division commanded by Major General Carter L. Stevenson to General Pemberton. Bragg did not want to part with these men because he knew he was already outnumbered by the U.S. forces under General William Rosecrans, who commanded forty-three thousand men, with another fifteen thousand in garrisons along the rail line that led to Louisville. Bragg had only forty-five thousand men on hand. The outcome of the meeting was never in doubt; rank would tell, and Davis held the higher rank, so Bragg accepted the decision with as much grace as he could muster.

The next presidential duty was more pleasant. Two officers had gained recent successes, and those were to be rewarded by promotions. Davis personally handed commissions as brigadier general to John Hunt Morgan and Roger W. Hanson in recognition of their victorious attack on Hartsville a few days earlier. At the same time, Patrick R. Cleburne was promoted to major general and put in command of the division formerly led by Simon Bolivar Buckner, who had just been transferred to East Tennessee.

No presidential visit would be complete without a review of troops, so the three divisions making up the corps of General Leonidas Polk were marched past the reviewing stand, where Davis and Bragg received their salutes. A few days later, Polk wrote to his wife, "The review was a grand affair, everything went off admirable, and he [Davis] was highly gratified with the result—said they were the best appearing troops he had seen, well appointed and well clad. The sight was very imposing and, as it was my corps, was very gratifying to me."[9] The *Murfreesboro Daily Rebel* said the troops were much impressed with Davis, who presented himself with "manly form" and an "unpretending style."[10] It is probably the case that most of the soldiers gave a sigh of relief when the whole thing was over, and they could return to their camps for a little relaxation.

Returning to Oaklands, a dinner was spread for Davis and the ranking generals of the army. As a finishing touch to the evening, a crowd of townspeople serenaded Davis, and he responded with a few remarks.

THE WEDDING

December 14, 1862, was a day the people around Murfreesboro would never forget. Often referred to as *the* social highlight of the Confederacy, everyone seemed happy when one of their own, the beautiful and charming Miss Martha Ready, became the bride of the dashing, daring cavalryman from Kentucky, General John Hunt Morgan.

Martha Ready Morgan, or "Mattie," as she was known to her friends, was a woman ahead of her time. She was the perfect match for the bold-riding general, and the "Thunderbolt of the Confederacy" was captured by her charms and fell in love. She discovered the kinder, gentler and very loving heart of this great cavalryman, and the intense love they shared would change both of their lives forever.

Martha Ready was born near Murfreesboro, Tennessee, on June 21, 1840, the child of Colonel Charles Ready Jr. and his wife, Martha Strong Ready. Mattie grew up in a privileged environment, attending the very prestigious Soule College in Murfreesboro and, during the 1850s, the Nashville Female Academy, where it was noted that young ladies could receive "traditional Southern education for women in cultural studies and social graces."[11] She was described as being a "very attractive young woman of medium height, with a shapely figure, a fair, creamy complexion, large blue eyes, and dark hair."[12]

Colonel Ready had served for a time as a U.S. Representative, and Mattie was known to be a favorite among Washington society, having many suitors both there and at home. She was considered to be "the first girl in Washington to wear a curl on her forehead, which was soon imitated by a hundred others,"[13] and was described as one of the "prettiest daughters of Old South society and a fashion trend-setter at eighteen."[14]

Captain John Hunt Morgan first arrived in the Middle Tennessee area in late February following the surrender of Nashville and set up camp headquarters near Murfreesboro. Charles Ready was known as a frequent visitor to local army camps, offering hospitality and support. After meeting Morgan, he invited him to dinner on March 2, 1862, and sent a slave home with word that "the famous Captain Morgan was coming. Tell Mattie that Captain Morgan is a widower and a little sad. I want her to sing for him."[15]

Morgan was a widower whose wife had been an invalid for many years. This had not prevented him from enjoying life, although he never did anything "which touched his integrity as a man and his honor as a gentleman."[16] Although Kentucky chose to remain neutral where the war issue was

Mattie Ready. *Library of Congress.*

concerned, Morgan aligned himself with other Southern sympathizers, and his militia unit, the Lexington Rifles, were among the first companies to join the newly created pro-Southern state militia. Early in 1862, Morgan's command became part of the thin screen thrown out to protect Johnston's army from Union attack on its retreat southward.

During the brief time Captain Morgan was in the Murfreesboro area, he made quite an impression on the lovely Mattie. They were obviously quite enamored with each other. When Morgan returned to Murfreesboro following an expedition to Gallatin and found a Union cavalry regiment conducting a reconnaissance outside the town, he sent Mattie a note inquiring as to whether the town was clear of Federals. "They are eight miles from here. Come in haste,"[17] was her hurried reply, which she handed to a courier, who returned to Morgan, ten miles to the north. A few hours later, in the early morning hours, Morgan appeared, and he and Mattie talked until daylight. Family tradition holds that they became engaged on that March 19. At dawn, John bade Mattie goodbye, forming his soldiers on the square and leading in the singing of "Cheer, Boys, Cheer."[18]

Late in the spring of 1862, Murfreesboro was under Federal rule. One day, as the spirited Mattie was crossing the street to her home, she heard some Union soldiers making disparaging remarks about Morgan. Perhaps this was an intentional effort on their part to "bait" her. She walked up to them and gave the Yankees a royal scolding, and when one of the soldiers asked her name, she replied, "It's Mattie Ready now! But by the grace of God, one day I hope to call myself the wife of John Morgan!"[19]

Morgan returned to the area during the autumn of 1862 and added to his fame. Probably one of the most unusual wedding presents in history resulted from Morgan's Raid on Hartsville, Tennessee, on December 7, 1862, when more than 1,800 Federal soldiers were captured. The shivering and bedraggled prisoners were then marched to Murfreesboro, and family lore credits the courtly Morgan as saying, "Mattie, here is my wedding gift to you, 1,200 Yankee prisoners of war."[20]

Sunday evening, December 14, 1862, Murfreesboro's own Southern belle, Miss Martha Strong Ready, and the handsome, newly promoted brigadier general from Kentucky, John Hunt Morgan, were united in matrimony. The wedding was held at the Ready home, across the street from the courthouse, facing East Main Street. It was described as a two-storied wooden structure, built in the 1850s, with a large hall and flanking parlors, one of which served as the scene for the wedding. Charles Ready's law office was in the east room on the ground floor. The house occupied the second lot of the block along East Main Street, the first lot being an ornamental garden with twin magnolia trees.

The wedding was perhaps the great social occasion of the Confederacy. Everybody who was anybody and could reach Murfreesboro in time was there. President Jefferson Davis had been in town just the day before.

Generals Bragg, Hardee, Cheatham and Breckinridge, including the headquarters staff, were all in attendance. Groomsmen were Mattie's brother, Horace Ready; an officer on General William J. Hardee's staff; and Colonel George St. Leger Grenfell, an English soldier of fortune. General Leonidas Polk, Episcopal bishop of the Diocese of Louisiana, nephew of former United States president James K. Polk and commander of a corps of Bragg's army encamped around Murfreesboro, performed the ceremony. Although raised in the Presbyterian Church, Mattie had converted to the Episcopalian faith just prior to her marriage. Morgan was not a particularly religious man at the time, but this was the faith of the Morgan family.

Years later, General Basil Duke, Morgan's brother-in-law and best friend who had served as Morgan's best man at the wedding, recalled in an August 31, 1912 interview with a *News-Banner* reporter in Louisville, Kentucky, his memories of that great celebration:

> *All the officers of high rank who could reach Murfreesboro had assembled for the wedding—General Bragg among them. Distinguished civilians were present in great numbers. The house was packed with people to its full capacity...and decorated with holly and winter berries. The lights from lamps and candles flashed on the uniforms and the trappings of the officers, and were reflected in the bright eyes of the pretty Tennessee girls who had gathered...The raven-haired, black-mustached Morgan, in his general's uniform, looking like a hero of chivalry, the bride, a girl of rare beauty, tall, dark-haired, and blue eyes, with a creamy complexion and perfect features, and standing before them, to perform the ceremony, in his full military uniform, Bishop Polk, himself a general of the Confederate Army, and Bishop of the Episcopal Church...Miss Ready's bridal dress was one of her best ante-bellum frocks, for it was not possible at that time to purchase material for a trousseau...General Duke was certain that the bride could not have worn anything more becoming. He remembers that she wore a bridal veil...General Morgan's attendants were as dashing a set of young soldiers as any bride could wish at her wedding...Two or three regimental bands had been provided for the occasion. They were stationed in the house and on the porch, and there was plenty of music. Outside in the streets thousands of soldiers were assembled, who by the lighted bonfires, celebrated the wedding proper style, cheering Morgan and his bride.*[21]

A Southern Wind Before Winter

Some of Morgan's men had speculated that they feared their general would put marriage first and career second, that marriage might slow him down. Colonel Grenfell had participated in the wedding but said later that he had attempted to prevent it, as he felt that marriage would cause John to become more cautious and less enterprising. Even Mattie's family had instructed her, "You must remember your promises, not to restrain the General in his career of glory, but encourage him to go forward."

A great supper was served in the Ready mansion after the wedding—turkeys, hams, chickens, ducks, game and all the delicacies and good dishes a Southern kitchen could produce, while the Ready wine cellar still had a sufficient stock to provide for the many toasts proposed to the happy couple. Following the wedding supper, the bands were called in, and the gallant soldiers and Tennessee belles danced to their hearts' content. Family legend holds that the general and his bride spent their first night of married life together at the Corners, the stately home built by Mattie's grandparents, Charles Ready Sr., a few miles east of town in Readyville. Their bedroom was upstairs, on the southeast corner of the house, with an outside entrance, and it had provided lodging over the years to such notables as Andrew Jackson, Martin Van Buren and James K. Polk.[22]

The next evening, Monday, December 15, 1862, the day after their wedding, a grand ball was held at the courthouse in honor of John and Mattie. Sponsored by the 1st Louisiana and the 6th Kentucky Regiments, candles illuminated the large hallways of the three-year-old courthouse, and behind each candle a bayonet reflected the light of the festive scene:

> *A pyramidal chandelier of bayonets and candles hung from the ceiling and trees of greenery and jars of flowers decorated the dance hall. Two B's, entwined in evergreen on one side of the hall, were representative of Bragg and Breckinridge, while trophies, including Yankee flags captured by Gen. John Hunt Morgan, were displayed. The revelers danced the stately cotillion and the graceful waltz far into the night, and one soldier later recalled, "The candle light shone on fair ladies and brave men."[23]*

One week after the wedding, General Morgan and Mattie rode off to Alexandria, Tennessee, and together they watched a grand parade of Morgan's troops. Everyone admired the handsome couple, and their obvious affection for each other was quite evident. The next day, December 22, 1862, eight days after their wedding, the newlyweds were separated when Morgan and his men rode north into Kentucky and Mattie returned to Murfreesboro. The happy couple, so much in love, could not know that their marriage would last only 630 days.[24] John Morgan was killed in Greenville, Tennessee, on September 4, 1864.

For Murfreesboro and its people, the good times were about to come to a screeching halt.

THE STORM BREAKS

The indications were obvious; a battle was imminent. William Starke Rosecrans was named to command the U.S. forces returning to Tennessee, and the new commander gave his army a new name: the Army of the Cumberland. From now on, the Yankees intended to stay. Rosecrans had his men ensconced in Nashville, only a few hours' march away. By mid-November, General Braxton Bragg had his army concentrated in Middle Tennessee in the vicinity of Murfreesboro and gave his force a new name: the Army of Tennessee. They were determined to defend their homes. Sharp clashes between cavalry forces became a daily occurrence, and infantry outposts had to remain on the alert constantly.

In mid-December, Forrest disappeared from the scene; when next heard of, he would be west of the Tennessee River, raiding and destroying the Memphis & Ohio Railroad, the lifeline of the army commanded by Ulysses Grant that was operating in Mississippi. Just a few days after the wedding, Morgan quietly rode out of town bound for the village of Alexandria. From there, he would launch his "Christmas Raid" into Kentucky to sever Rosecrans's supply line, the L&N Railroad. Wheeler would keep his cavalry corps on the move covering the roads south out of Nashville and, on December 26, would report that those roads were full of blue infantry coming toward Murfreesboro. The storm of battle was about to break over the town.

Preparations were made. Soldiers who were sick were evacuated from the established hospitals at Union University and Soule College to make room for wounded, and the sick were sent to hospitals in Shelbyville, Tullahoma and Winchester. Public buildings, including churches, were cleared of furnishings, and straw was put on the floor to receive casualties. Troop positions were chosen, and fields of fire were cleared. This meant that some families found themselves living on the anticipated battlefield, and they had to evacuate while their outbuildings were burned or torn down. In at least one case, the fire spread to the dwelling of the Cowan family, and their large brick house was destroyed. Each day, the reports from the army told of skirmishing between Wheeler and the advance guard of the Army of the Cumberland, and each day the fighting was closer to town.

In the pre-dawn hours of December 31, 1862, the first shots were fired. The Army of Tennessee struck first, hitting and rolling back the right wing of Rosecrans's force. The initial success slowed as the day went on, but by the end of the day it appeared that a victory was within grasp of the Confederates. A local observer said:

William S. Rosecrans. *Library of Congress.*

Being a clear, bright morning, the sun rising without a cloud to obscure, a frost the over night, mild weather to the feelings. It would seem that all nature was rejoicing after so many days of having been shrouded in clouds but there is about to be the roar of cannon, the clash of arms, the dead and the dying. The cannonading was, at first, at intervals. In a very short time became furious. The musketry peal after peal.[25]

In Murfreesboro, it was clear that this had not been achieved without the shedding of blood. Many of the civilians in the town were ready to do what they could to relieve the suffering, so the front page of the *Daily Rebel Banner* for January 1, 1863, carried a list of hospitals and the commands with which they were associated:

Wither's Division, Baptist Female Institute
Cheatham's Division, Soule Female College
McCown's Division, Old Academy

Wood's Brigade, Methodist Church
Johnson's Brigade, Presbyterian Church
Polk's Brigade, Baptist Church
Liddel's Brigade, Old Presbyterian Church
Hanson's Brigade, City Hotel
Palmer's Brigade, Dr. January's
Adam's Brigade, On Liberty Pike[26]

Each hospital served men from the division or brigade listed, information urgently desired by the people of Murfreesboro because every one of the Confederate units raised in the town was present on the battlefield. The men and boys of the town were fighting in the shadow of their own homes.

The second day of the battle was strangely quiet, both on the field and in the town. The news of a Yankee retreat was expected momentarily, but no such news came. Instead, the wounded continued to arrive at the hospitals. Across the river, those who could get high enough to view the scene could see long lines of wagons moving toward Nashville carrying the U.S. wounded able to make the trip to hospitals in Nashville.

Cannon at Stones River. *Authors' collection.*

The third day of the conflict, January 2, brought a short but deadly burst of fighting that taxed the hospitals of the town to their capacity. An attack on the Confederate right led hundreds of Kentucky and Tennessee soldiers into a devastating artillery barrage with enormous casualties. One of them was Captain Spencer Talley, of the 28th Tennessee, who was taken from the field to a hospital that had been established in the courthouse. As he lay awaiting medical attention, he saw the body of his commanding officer, Colonel Peter Davidson Cunningham. Talley wrote:

> *When his body was brought in the hospital my heart was full of sorrow and, regardless of my wound, I secured a vessel of water and washed his blood-stained head, face, and hands. The coat which I had worn a few nights before to the grand ball and festival were now stained with his life's blood. I removed the stains from his coat as best I could with cold water and a rag, combed his unkempt hair and whiskers and laid his body with many others in the courthouse in Murfreesboro.*[27]

This regiment was part of Palmer's Brigade and included many local men.

The scenes one saw in the hospitals were never to be forgotten. One account concerning the Hord House, which was used as a field hospital by the U.S. Army before it was overrun and used by the Confederates, could be used to describe many others:

> *Human limbs and pieces of flesh were cast outside of the house, through the windows, and the amount would have filled a cart. The floors of the premises ran rivers of blood, and the surgeons and attendants, in their long dress, resembled butchers at work in the shambles. The long line of graves, both Union and Rebels, now coursing down the sloping field behind the house attest the many sad results of battle.*[28]

The mother and wife of two men on the field was a local resident named Rebecca Ridley. She went into Murfreesboro on the afternoon of January 3 to look for her husband and son and was just in time to witness the aftermath of the attack made by the Confederates at that time:

> *On entering town what a sight met my eyes! Prisoners entering every street, ambulances bringing in the wounded, every place crowded with the dying, the Federal general, Sill, lying dead in the courthouse—killed Wednesday—Frank Crosthwaite's lifeless corpse stretched on a counter. He had been visiting my*

home and was killed on Wednesday. The churches were full of wounded where the doctors were amputating arms and legs. I found my own safe, and being informed that another battle was expected to begin, I set off on my way home, and passed through our cavalry drawn up in a line. I had only gone a mile when the first cannon boomed, but I was safe.[29]

Not all seekers found such a happy end to their search. The parents of Monroe Bearden had traveled from Fayetteville, some thirty miles, to look for their son:

Jan. 2, 1863. Found Monroe in the Soule Female College which was made use of for Cheatham's Division hospital. At which place hundreds of our poor boys lay wounded in every conceivable manner.
Jan. 3, 1863. Monroe seems to be doing well, many deaths among the wounded. Moved Monroe to the room which I rented he seemed quite comfortable after the change of quarters.

The parents stayed with their son even when the Army of Tennessee left Murfreesboro. On January 20, the father recorded:

Monroe much worse. I lost all hope of his recovery. O God who could describe my feelings just to think of giving up my dear boy. About 11 or 12 O'clock P.M. I told my dear boy that he was doomed to die, he said that he was not aware of it. Asked how long he had to live, I told him I did not know—that death was not on him at that time—he seems perfectly resigned to his fate. O God, this is the hardest trial of my life.
Jan. 21, 1863. But little change in Monroe. Monroe called me about 11 O'clock P.M. On being asked what he wanted he said morphine. I gave him morphine, he went to sleep.
Jan. 22, 1863. 4:00 O'clock 20 min A.M. Died in the north end room of Dr. Tompkins residence Murfreesboro, Tenn. Capt. Napoleon Monroe Bearden, Capt. Of Co. E, 8th Tenn. Volunteers.[30]

On the battlefield, the fight was a draw. Rosecrans was many miles from Nashville, with only a tenuous supply line, but Bragg was not confident he could hold his position either. The will to continue the confrontation collapsed in Bragg's mind first, and on January 4, the decision was reached to retreat. John Spence observed the movement:

Monroe Bearden. *Courtesy of the Bearden family.*

Saturday evening General Bragg commenced his retreat from this place, all his army stores having been sent off by rail road during the week with the exception of enough for present purposes. His wagons, loaded with all his camp equipage, out on the road, ready for orders...His men all fell back, in good order, every thing was in motion. The retreat was quiet and undisturbed.[31]

On January 5, the Army of the Cumberland took possession of Murfreesboro. The end of the battle was only the beginning of the fight for the surviving wounded.

Captain Philip Welshimer, of the 21st Illinois, said, "In Murfreesboro every house is a hospital mostly filled with the worst wounded rebels...there is from five to seven thousand of them. In fact every house through this country is filled with their sick and wounded." Another U.S. soldier, Ira M.B. Gillespie, of the 11th Michigan, wrote:

I was detailed corporal of the burial guard. We buried 27 dead bodys and one extra leg and three arms. The wounded men are dieing off very fast now. Confederate nurse James Searcy told of the women of the town's

involvement: The ladies are untiring in their exertions for our wounded…
James Maxwell and I are of great value here, even or inexperienced services.
Nurses are scarce, hardly enough to bury the dead…The enemy have treated
us well so far.[32]

Not all the women were local. Ann Hosner of the United States Sanitary Commission stared south from Chicago as soon as she heard of the battle beginning. She arrived in Nashville on January 3 but had to wait for an armed escort to guard her against guerrillas on the road to Murfreesboro. Upon reaching the battlefield, she found the U.S. wounded had been moved from the tents of field hospitals to deserted houses. She immediately set up a kitchen, drew army rations and began to prepare food for the patients. Each day, she sliced and toasted twenty loaves of bread, stewed a barrel of dried apples to make applesauce, made endless kettles of soup and provided eggnog and milk punch. She remained in Murfreesboro for eleven weeks.[33]

Bettie Ransom of Murfreesboro wrote to her brother, who was in the Confederate army:

It makes one sick at heart to think of the pain and devastation by this
miserable war on our country, the sacrifice of so many precious lives and the
desolation of so many homes and the untold agony of numbers of widows,
mothers, and orphans but there is a God of justice that will avenge the right.
By the bravery of our noble soldiers and the power of an almighty hand the
South will triumph.[34]

Faith in God, and much more, would be needed to sustain the people of Murfreesboro as stormy weather settled over their town. It would last more than two years.

5

Stormy Weather

The great battle was over, the Confederate army had departed, the town was crowded with wounded men and those who nursed them, the Emancipation Proclamation had gone into effect and, even though Tennessee was not included in the proclamation's coverage, a new age had dawned for the African American population of Murfreesboro and of the nation. All these changes would have social as well as military and political implications. The coming days would be characterized by stormy weather no matter what the season of the year.

An Enormous Work

Murfreesboro was not a comfortable place for the Yankees. Just as before, they found themselves dangling at the end of a long, tenuous supply line. In 1862, Morgan and Forrest had made life miserable for the occupiers, smashing the railroad, ambushing forage parties and even raiding the town and capturing the garrison. During the battle along the banks of Stones River, the Rebel cavalry under Joseph Wheeler had circled the Yankees' rear twice, burning trains of supply wagons and leaving it an open question as to which side would find it necessary to retreat.

The situation had not improved. The Confederate success in defeating Grant's drive on Vicksburg had allowed Richmond to bring Earl Van Dorn's cavalry up from Mississippi so that Bragg had sixteen thousand horsemen under the best-known and most successful cavalry commanders in the western area of the war. The Army of the Cumberland occupied the battlefield, but the supply of beans and bullets was far from certain. If Rosecrans was to keep what he had won, much less move forward, the logistics problem had to be solved and a secure base of supply established. The solution was a good engineer, thousands of men to dig and tons of timber and dirt. An enormous amount of work was about to begin.

The chief engineer of the Army of the Cumberland was Brigadier General James S. Morton, and the task of designing a fortification to protect the supply base fell to him. Since the supply situation combined with the winter weather would prevent movement by the army for several months, General Morton decided to think big. He chose a site covering two hundred acres on the western side of the town, land belonging to two prominent pro-Confederate families, the Lytles and the Maneys, and began to draw up his plans. Soon, he had designed an earthen fort running 1,250 yards north to south and 1,070 yards east to west. In all, the circumference of the fortification would be more than two miles. The outer line would consist of "lunettes," earthworks shaped something like an arrowhead spaced a few hundred yards apart but connected by "curtain walls"—breast-high mounds of dirt behind which infantry could take cover. Each lunette would hold field artillery placed to fire parallel to the curtain walls. Outside the curtain walls and lunette line would be a ditch six feet deep and six feet across. Beyond the ditch, all timber, brush and high grass would be cut or burned to clear a field of fire for 1,450 yards.

Inside the outer line was a series of four redoubts, large rectangular earthworks in which artillery of large caliber would be mounted. Some of these guns would be eight inches in diameter, while others would fire shells weighing sixty-four pounds. Each of these redoubts was designed to stand alone should the outer curtain wall be breached by an attack or even if one of the other redoubts should be captured. There were three "demilunes," semicircular earthworks, outside the curtain walls to protect the railroad as it entered and exited the fort and one to guard the Nashville Pike. Dirt began to fly and axes to ring on January 23, 1863, with work details being drawn from each infantry unit in turn and hundreds of African American men hired as laborers to assist in the work. Construction went on twenty-four hours a day, seven days a week, with up to seven thousand men at work at any given time.[1] John Spence described what the work looked like to the townspeople. "Large quantities of timber trees are cut and hauled to the grounds. The work is commenced and pushed on vigorously—digging and blasting rocks. A great number of negros are employed at this kind of work, under pay, of course."[2]

Fort Rosecrans was not just for defense; it was intended to be the main army base and supply depot for the forward movement of the U.S. forces in Middle Tennessee. As such, it was designed to house fifty thousand men with enough supplies to last ninety days. Inside the walls were three commissary depots, a quartermaster depot, two ordnance depots, an engineering depot, an artillery depot and four sawmills. The tracks of the N&C passed through the fortification, so loading and unloading cars could be done in a secure location.[3] When sawed lumber or brick was needed for construction in the fort, the source was often a building in Murfreesboro. Members of the Pioneer Brigade, or construction troops, would select a building and then proceed to dismantle it, even if it were inhabited. Planks were ripped off dwellings to floor tents, and fences became firewood. The Presbyterian church was first a hospital, then a storehouse and then a stable and then was torn down, with the brick used to construct ovens to bake bread for the garrison of Fort Rosecrans.[4]

By March 1863, the works were complete enough that the camps of several units were moved inside the walls. When the Army of the Cumberland left on June 24 to begin the Tullahoma Campaign, those troops remaining as a garrison were housed in barracks in the fort. After all the work expended, the site would see combat only once in December 1864, and that was outside the fortified area.

BLOOD AND FIRE

"Blood and fire are the methods I use, I shoot the men and burn their houses." These words are part of a letter Major General Robert Milroy, U.S. Army, wrote to his wife in 1864. Milroy was the commanding officer of the provost marshal troops that occupied Military Sub-District #1, Defenses of the Nashville & Chattanooga Railroad, an area stretching from Murfreesboro to Bridgeport, Alabama. Milroy issued official orders for the arrest and execution without trial of over five hundred citizens of the area, but he did not quench the ardor of those who were pro-Confederate. The area under his control came to swarm with guerrillas and became a cockpit of war.[5]

The story of the entire area is illustrated by the account of one family from the vicinity of Murfreesboro.

Three Cousins:
Thomas Benton Smith, DeWitt Smith Jobe and DeWitt Smith

The Civil War was a family affair. Three young men, first cousins, entered into it with great enthusiasm and high expectations for a Southern victory. All met tragic and horrible deaths at the hands of Federal troops.

The oldest of the cousins, Benton Smith, was a natural leader and rose from lieutenant to brigadier general by age twenty-six, thus becoming the youngest general in the Confederate army. DeWitt Smith Jobe, the next oldest, would become a scout and spy, delivering valuable information behind enemy lines and well known for his bravery. DeWitt, or "Dee," Smith was the youngest, the "wild one," known for his love of a good fight and extreme hatred of Yankees.

Thomas Benton Smith was born near Mechanicsville on February 24, 1838, and attended local schools. He was considered to be a very bright young man with a gift for mechanical inventiveness. At age fifteen, he was granted a patent for a locomotive pilot, the device mounted on the front of a train to deflect obstacles from the track, better known as the "cowcatcher." The next year, he was a student at Western Military Institute in Nashville and, upon graduation, was given an appointment to the United States Military Academy. Tom only attended West Point for a short time, however, before he resigned. He came home and subsequently went to work for the Nashville & Decatur Railroad.

At the outbreak of war, Tom was twenty-three and enlisted in the Zollicoffer Guards of the 20th Tennessee Regiment. Both Tom and his brother John were privates in Company B, but Tom was soon promoted to second lieutenant, where he first saw combat at the Battle of Fishing Creek in January 1862 and then again in April at Shiloh, where the regiment lost 187 men, either killed or wounded, out of approximately 400. When the company regrouped at Corinth, Mississippi, Smith was promoted to colonel and assigned command of a small brigade. The regiment was now in John C. Breckinridge's Division and spent the remainder of the summer in Mississippi and Louisiana before returning to Tennessee in the fall of 1862.

Colonel Smith led his men bravely at the Battle of Stones River on December 31, 1862, and was shot through the breast and left arm, serious wounds that would render him incapacitated for most of 1863. W.J. McMurray recalled:

Stormy Weather

Three cousins, *left to right*: DeWitt Smith Jobe, Thomas Benton Smith and DeWitt Smith. *Courtesy of John Bridges.*

> *We formed in an open field, and moved forward under heavy shelling until we struck a picket fence. Only the Twentieth Tennessee Regiment came into contact with that fence, when Colonel T.B. Smith gave the command, "By the right flank, tear down that picket fence, March!" This command caused a great deal of laughter among the boys of his Regiment, but it was the last laugh that many of these brave fellows ever had.*[6]

Smith returned to field duty and was at Chickamauga in September 1863. Wounded once more—shot in the arm—he was able to fight at Missionary Ridge, and when the brigade commander, Brigadier General B.C. Tyler, was wounded, Smith assumed command. He would lead the brigade throughout the Atlanta Campaign in 1864. On July 29, 1864, Tom received his commission as brigadier general, making him the youngest brigadier in the Army of Tennessee and earning the nickname of the "Boy General."

Smith led his men from Atlanta back to Tennessee and the ill-fated Battle of Franklin on November 30, 1864, where his good friend Captain Tod Carter was fatally wounded. The next morning, he rode to the Carter house nearby, informed the family of Tod's fate and then led them to Tod on the battlefield. After Franklin, the division was ordered to Murfreesboro, home to many of the men, some of whom "took French leave" and did not return. What was left of the brigade was ordered to Nashville. Smith's military career ended at the Battle of Nashville on December 16, 1864, shortly after 4:00 p.m. After two days of heavy losses, greatly outnumbered, Smith pulled a small white handkerchief from his pocket, waved it over his head and ordered his men to cease-fire. After surrender, as he was being led to the rear, Smith was confronted by Colonel William Linn McMillan of the 95th Ohio Infantry, who cursed and berated him. Smith's only response, according to witnesses, was to state, "I am a disarmed prisoner," which further infuriated the already enraged, and most likely drunk, McMillan, "who drew his saber and struck Smith three times over the head, each blow cutting through Smith's hat and crashing into his skull."[7] Federal officers, shocked at the actions of their own officer, rushed Smith to a field hospital, where he was told by an attending physician, "Well, you are near the end of your battles, for I can see the brain oozing through the gap in your skull."[8] The Boy General surprised his captors by recovering and was considered well enough to be sent on to prison at Fort Warren, Massachusetts, where he would remain until being paroled at the end of the war.

Returning to Nashville, Smith went back to work for the railroad and then ran an unsuccessful race for the U.S. Congress in 1870. He would suffer from periods of intense clinical depression, which ultimately left him unable to live on his own, and in 1876, he was admitted to the Tennessee State Asylum, where he would spend the majority of the remainder of his life. He never forgot his men of the 20th Tennessee, and they did not forget him. He was able to attend a reunion in 1897 and again a few years later when he was seventy-two years old:

At a recent reunion of the 20th Tennessee Regiment at Nashville, Tenn… Gen. Thomas Benton Smith was in command for a drill and short parade. The regiment was formed as a company, and the drill master, though now somewhat venerable…carried the men through the manual of Hardee's tactics as if half a century were half a year. General Smith was self-poised, as full of the animation of the old days as could be imagined.[9]

Thomas Benton Smith died from a heart condition on May 21, 1923, at age eighty-six. He is buried at Confederate Circle in Mount Olivet Cemetery in Nashville. The Boy General had outlived all but two Confederate generals.

While the fate of Thomas Benton Smith was indeed a sad one, that which befell his cousin DeWitt Smith Jobe was much more horrific. Dewitt Smith Jobe was born near Mechanicsville on June 4, 1840, the son of a farmer and cabinetmaker known for the fine coffins he made. On May 27, 1861, at College Grove, Jobe enlisted in Company D, 20th Tennessee Infantry Regiment, as a private, seeing his first action at the Battle of Fishing Creek, Kentucky, where he was wounded and captured on January 19, 1862. He was sent to the Federal prison at Camp Chase, Ohio, and remained there until late August, when he was exchanged. He rejoined his command prior to the Battle of Murfreesboro.

In April 1863, with Bragg's army encamped at Shelbyville, Jobe was detached by General William J. Hardee to perform dangerous scouting duties in and around Yankee-occupied territory. When Bragg's army fell back into Georgia later that summer, Jobe did not retreat with the rest of the army but stayed near his home turf, now as a member of the famed, select, hand-picked young men known as the "Coleman Scouts."

During 1864, the Coleman Scouts were still operating in Middle Tennessee, although several had been killed or imprisoned. Although it was unclear to whom the scouts were now reporting, they continued to move in and out of occupied Nashville, gathering information and collecting supplies, horses, guns, medicine and anything else that might prove useful. During late summer, DeWitt Jobe was scouting around the areas of College Grove, Triune and Nolensville even though the Federals in Nashville were suspicious and knew that he had a hiding place somewhere in the area.

On the night of August 29, 1864, Jobe rode all night and, about sunrise the next morning, reached the home of William Moss on the Nolensville Pike, about halfway between Nolensville and Triune, a house he knew to be safe. But when daylight came, he left the Moss home and went about one mile west to the Sam Waters farm, where he concealed himself and his horse in a cornfield. While there are varying accounts of DeWitt Smith Jobe's last hours, perhaps one of the most factual and detailed reports is from a letter written by H.E. Jobe of Paris, Tennessee, a nephew of Jobe, and published in the December 1895 *Confederate Veteran* magazine:

> *On one of these scouts he went to the house of Sam Waters, between Triune and Nolensville, where he met his true and tried friend, Miss Bettie Puckett, who frequently gave him information in regard to the enemy's movement. She directed him to a thicket near by to remain during the day, where she could furnish him food for himself and horse. He was gone only a short time when a squad of Federal cavalry came up in pursuit of him and accused Miss Bettie of concealing him. She endeavored to decoy them in a different direction, but seeing the tracks of his horse, they soon found him asleep in the thicket.*[10]

Jobe found himself surrounded by a fifteen-man mounted patrol from the 115th Ohio. Knowing that the papers he carried, if taken, would have condemned himself and others, he did the only thing he could: He tore and then chewed the papers until they were illegible. Then he swallowed them. This infuriated the men of this 115th Ohio under the command of Sergeant Temple, so they did not take Jobe back to Nashville but chose instead to try to make him divulge the contents of the papers he had destroyed. Jobe continually refused:

> *Then they tied a leather strap around his neck and began to choke him to death, but the brave boy in gray, who was alone, disarmed, and both hands tied, with fifteen of his armed enemies standing over him thirsting for his blood, would not concede to their demands. Jobe, in this condition, chose not to betray his friends or to divulge his secret but preferred death. The captors beat him over the head with their guns, knocked out his upper front teeth, and dragged him by the leather strap that they had placed about his neck until he was strangled to death.*[11]

A letter from Mrs. J.T. McCarthy, a niece of DeWitt Smith Jobe, provided the following details of her uncle's capture and death:

> *They demanded the secret information which he had, and upon his refusal to divulge it, they first threatened him, then began to torture him, trying to force him to tell the secret which he was carrying. Finally they told him that if he would not tell what they wanted to know, they would cut out his tongue. He still refused and they did cut out his tongue.*[12]

Miss Jeanette King of Murfreesboro recalled this tragedy:

> *After Dee Jobe had refused repeatedly to divulge the contents of the papers and the name of the person giving them to him, the Yankees proceeded to torture him. They beat out his teeth with the butt of a pistol, punched out his eyes with a bayonet, and finally after Jobe showered them with epithets, they cut out his tongue. Not satisfied with this they choked him to death with a rope.*[13]

The fifteen savages from this 115th Ohio seemed to enjoy what they were doing. "The torture went on. The Yanks were whooping now, yelling so loudly that they could be heard at a distant farmhouse."[14] Finally, the dastardly deed was done, and the life of DeWitt Smith Jobe, at age twenty-four, was over.

When word reached Jobe's home, only six miles away, of what had happened, Frank, the old Negro servant who had cared for him as a child, took the wagon and brought Jobe's body home. He was buried in the family cemetery.

This shameful event is not mentioned in the official records of the Union army. It is, however, preserved in Jobe family history, letters and books. It was later said that this cruel and inhumane act preyed on the mind of Sergeant Temple and that he eventually went insane and became a "raving maniac." Temple did not die until 1919, and the only suffering mentioned in his pension application was from rheumatism, for which he was hospitalized in the spring of 1865.

While justice was not served in regard to DeWitt Smith Jobe, there was revenge. And revenge came in the person of the youngest, the wildest, the self-appointed avenging cousin known as DeWitt, or Dee, Smith.

Dee Smith was born in 1842, the son of Alexander and Clara Smith. In the fall of 1861, he joined Company D, 45th Tennessee Infantry Regiment, as a private. In April, Dee fought bravely at the Battle of Shiloh, and when the company reorganized, he was elected first corporal on May 19, 1862. He went on to participate at the Battle of Baton Rouge and then returned home for the Battle of Stones River. September 1863 found Smith at Chattanooga, serving under Colonel Anderson Searcy of Murfreesboro, who was in command of the 45th, and it was near here that he was captured on September 11, 1863. Records of the 45th Infantry Regiment show Smith as having deserted on September 8, 1863, and then as being a prisoner of war. (This was not unusual since many Southern soldiers were shown as deserters when in fact they were prisoners of war.) Less than two weeks later, on September 20, Smith took the oath of allegiance at Stevenson, Alabama. There is no mention of Dee Smith until the next year, when he learned of his cousin's brutal murder, at which time he raised the "black flag," swearing to kill any Yankee who crossed his path. This path apparently began at Tullahoma a few nights later, when Smith slipped into the sleeping camp of a small company of Yankee cavalry and used a large butcher knife to slit the throats of fourteen Union soldiers while they slept. His intended would-be fifteenth victim awakened, sounding the alarm. Smith managed to escape. According to an account given years later by one of the remaining Confederate veterans in Rutherford County, ninety-seven-year-old Sam Mitchell:

He found his horse...and rode madly out the road to Murfreesboro. The Yankee pursuers said that Smith still carried a big bloody butcher knife as he rode, waving it menacingly in their direction. Somewhere past Manchester Smith eluded his enemies and before many hours was in Rutherford County.[15]

Smith continued on this personal vendetta for almost two months, killing as many as fifty enemy soldiers. He developed an intense hatred for Union sympathizers, particularly those who had taken the oath of allegiance to the United States. During this time, he hid out in the woods close to his home near the place where Jobe was killed, and friends and family supplied him with food and a bed for the night. He was considered a hero by some, a villain by others and feared by most. Separating fact from fiction is an almost impossible task, but there is no doubt that Smith was obviously the target of many rumors, some exaggerated truths and even a few unintentional mistakes.[16]

Smith was finally captured near Nolensville, and according to Murfreesboro's John Cedric Spence, his capture began with the killing in cold blood of an old man thought to be an informant:

Smith called at the house of an old man named "B"...deliberately shooting and killing him dead. Several shots were fired all taking effect. The family is then ordered to leave the house immediately. Fire is placed to the building. It burns to the ground...It appeared the old man was styled a union man...giving information to the authorities in town... The body of the dead man was taken to a son-in-law for burial... the undertaker...making preparation for internment...Smith rides up... walks in...going to where the dead man lay, he deliberately turns him about to examine where he had shot him...then calling for wood, with an oath sweating he will burn him up, ordering all out of the house. In the mean time a neighbor man came in, contending it shall not be done. The man was finally put in proper condition and buried...Young Smith, still roaming about the neighborhood, a terror to many, giving out word he will retaliate on any one who may interfere...Two young men wishing to take him for the Yankees...pretending to be friends...proposed they take a ride. After going some distance on the road...demand him to surrender... he refused...drawing a pistol, shot one of the friends...the other firing at Smith, wounding in the face. He fell from his horse...the one firing last fled, returning to town, [Nolensville] secreting himself in a house. Smith...recovers sufficiently...returns to the same place, commencing a search for the man that shot him. Finding the whereabouts, walks in and commences firing at and wounding him. Then taking fire for the purpose of burning the house, which was…prevented…he threatening to shoot any one that would stop him. The woman of the house begging him not to fire it. Some person from the opposite street with a double barrel shot gun, fired a load buck shot at him, mortally wounding him.[17]

Bromfield Ridley stated:

It is asserted that he slew not less than fifty of his enemies. At last they surrounded him near Nolensville, Tennessee, and shot him. Afterwards they brought him twenty miles from Nolensville to Murfreesboro. Although in excruciating pain when the doctors probed his wounds, he said that he would die before his enemies should see him flinch. Fortunately, he died before noon of the next day, at which time he was to be hanged.[18]

The exact date of Smith's death and place of burial are unknown. John Cedric Spence had this to say about the mortally wounded Smith after his capture:

[He was] *brought to Murfreesboro in a dying condition. He lived about three days after and died, his wounds being greatly aggravated…It was not certain what would be done with him. There were various reports about the streets. One, on the Monday following he would be taken out and hung… the Yankees were so much exasperated at him they were ready to commit almost any act, even to hang a half killed man…The relations of the young man were not permitted to see him when alive. He was kept in the court house until his death. His remains were given to friends, taken home and buried…Thus, ends the life of one of the most reckless, daring young men of the age.*[19]

BOTTOM RAIL ON TOP?

Times would have been hard in Murfreesboro even without the presence of guerrillas and vindictive provost marshals. Crime became prevalent because there were no civil authorities, and the U.S. military presence was largely limited to the town, leaving the rural areas in a lawless condition. Food prices rose as much of the local farm produce was seized by the military for use by the army. The countryside for miles around town had been stripped of timber, leaving firewood for heating and cooking a scarce and expensive commodity. Fences disappeared into the fireplaces of homes and bivouacs, while empty buildings lost siding boards and then structural timbers. Although the U.S. garrison moved to barracks in Fort Rosecrans, the streets of town were crowded with military vehicles and with soldiers who simply wandered away from their camps without a pass. Many of these men brought weapons with them, leading to incidents of armed robbery against civilians.

Quite troublesome to the residents was the presence of large numbers of refugees, white and black, who had come to find protection and food. These people had no work but received rations from the government. The refugees took over churches and other public spaces or built shanties on empty lots. They cooked in the street and created sanitation problems that the town could not handle. Not surprisingly, there was friction between the white population and the African Americans whose legal and social status was vague.

Tennessee was not included in the provisions of the Emancipation Proclamation, so there was not even the thin legal protection of that document for the black population. The presence of the U.S. Army did mean that steps would be taken to ensure that the labor of black men and women did not support the Confederate war effort or contribute to the income of pro-Confederates. While the white soldiers in the Union ranks, as a rule, shared the common nineteenth-century prejudices concerning race, the men had become "pragmatic abolitionists" who felt that ending slavery would weaken the South and speed the end of the war. An African American approaching a U.S. soldier did not know if he would be met with blessings or blows, but he did know he would not be considered a slave. The "bottom rail was not on top," but the bottom rail was moving. A social revolution was taking place in Murfreesboro and across the nation.

In Murfreesboro, many African Americans found employment with the U.S. Army as laborers and teamsters, or in the case of women, as laundresses or cooks, but others preferred the familiar surroundings of the white family, where they had worked all their lives, and remained with them—although with a newfound sense of limited, but growing, independence.

The most obvious symbol of the changes taking place was the appearance of black men in blue uniforms. The decision to enlist African Americans as soldiers was reached for a number of reasons, some noble and some pragmatic. If the Emancipation Proclamation said that black people behind Confederate lines were free, the implication was that slavery behind Union lines was a dead issue; black people could choose their own course, which might include military service. Although no white men from the North wanted to serve in the ranks with black men—belief in white superiority was the accepted point of view in both America and Europe—there was a growing belief that if a war was to be fought to benefit the black race, some of the blood shed should come from black bodies. In short, principle and pragmatism indicated that African Americans should be soldiers.

In Tennessee, Colonel Reuben D. Mussey was the agent who put this decision into practice. Before the war, Mussey was a prominent lawyer and a supporter of Lincoln in the 1860 election. An abolitionist by conviction, the colonel was put in charge of recruiting for the newly authorized United States Colored Troops (USCT). In this capacity, a training camp, called Camp Mussey, was established at Nashville, and in July recruiters showed up in Murfreesboro. The process of recruiting was sped by General Order #5, issued by Brigadier General J.D. Morgan on August 6, 1863. This order mandated that "all Negroes employed as teamsters and cooks will be mustered and enrolled." By November 1863, enough men had been enlisted to form a regiment, which would be designated the 13th USCT, an infantry unit.

This regiment was presented a regimental flag, blue with the U.S. coat of arms, embroidered with the words: "Presented by the Colored Ladies of Murfreesboro."[20] This regiment spent most of its time guarding the Nashville & Northwest Railroad, but it came under fire when Bedford Forrest raided Johnsonville, Tennessee, and it was heavily engaged in combat at the Battle of Nashville.

Murfreesboro's citizens also had a great deal of contact with the 111th USCT. This regiment was raised in the vicinity of Pulaski but was stationed in Murfreesboro toward the end of the fighting. The major activity of this regiment while at Murfreesboro was its work on the National Cemetery.

It should be remembered that at Murfreesboro, as was the case all over the South, African Americans were drafted for military service as well as volunteering. Major General Lovell Rousseau commented from his headquarters in Nashville on January 30, 1864, that "officers in command of colored troops are in constant habit of pressing all able bodied slaves into the military service of the United States."[21] Change would not be smooth or easy, but change was arriving for the African American residents of Murfreesboro.

MONUMENTS AND CEMETERIES

During the fighting around Murfreesboro at the end of December and the first days of January 1862–63, the men of both armies were usually hastily buried where they fell. Impromptu burial places were established at the site of hospitals. The soldiers of Hazen's Brigade of the Army of the Cumberland did collect their dead in the Round Forest area of the battlefield and bury them in an orderly fashion, erecting a large stone monument to their memory, a monument that is still a landmark at Stones River National Battlefield. The graves of the rest of the dead, blue and gray, were left unattended. As early as 1862, an act of the U.S. Congress ordered that national cemeteries be created for the decent burial of U.S. dead. General George Thomas ordered General Horatio Van Cleve, the commanding officer at Murfreesboro, to have such a cemetery created, and Captain John A. Means, of the 115th Ohio, was ordered to choose a location. The site Means picked was a knoll on the battlefield where two gun batteries had helped defend the Round Forest area and fired on Confederates as they advanced across the Cotton Field. Later, a blockhouse had been erected on this spot to protect the railroad. At first, local citizens were forced to work without pay to clear the blockhouse and prepare the land for use. In June 1865, Captain Means was mustered out of service, and Chaplain William Earnshaw became the superintendent of the proposed cemetery. With the assistance of the 111th USCT, the process of moving bodies to the chosen location was begun.[22]

Earnshaw had enlisted as a private in the 49th Pennsylvania Infantry but had been appointed chaplain of the regiment. He became hospital chaplain in 1863 and continued serving until 1867. In the course of his work, he would lay out the national cemeteries at Murfreesboro, Nashville, Fort Donelson, Shiloh, Corinth and Memphis. One obstacle facing Earnshaw was the owner of the land chosen for the burials. Benjamin Lillard was a strong Confederate, and he refused to sell his land for the burial of Yankees, even when offered the astronomical price of eighty dollars an acre. While the legal issues were being worked out, Earnshaw and the 111th USCT began moving bodies in October 1865. First, graves on the battlefield were located and examined, and U.S. dead were moved to the chosen location. Hospital deaths from Murfreesboro were next to be exhumed and reburied. Then an area between the Nashville Pike and Stones River was cleared of graves, followed by removals of the dead men from Forrest's 1862 raid who had been interred in the city cemetery. The area along Sevier Street

Hazen Monument. *Photo by authors.*

to Monroe Street out to the Woodbury Pike was found to contain several hundred corpses. Over three thousand bodies were exhumed from the area around the buildings of Union University. Hoovers Gap, Liberty Gap and Guys Gap were then searched for dead from the Tullahoma Campaign, with six hundred bodies being found at Sewanee on the campus of the University of the South.[23]

All the remains were placed in wooden coffins with whatever information was available recorded on the lids. About 25 percent of the remains were marked "unknown." In addition to carrying out the gruesome task of finding, disinterring and recovering the remains, the soldiers of the 111th USCT built the first stone wall around the cemetery. While this process was going on, Lillard died, and his estate was turned over to clerk and master James M. Tompkins, who sold twenty acres to the U.S. government for a total of $599.50.

The National Cemetery was not popular with the pro-Confederate citizens of the area for the simple reason that their dead were excluded from burial in its precincts, although their tax dollars helped maintain the graves of those they viewed as "invaders." Also, the Memorial Day commemorations

Stones River National Cemetery. *Photo by authors.*

were an occasion for solemn celebration of the sacrifices that achieved the Union victory, as well as a jubilant celebration of emancipation by the African American population.[24]

The Confederate dead were not forgotten by their people. On May 27, 1865, the Murfreesboro Memorial Association was formed by Charles Ready, John Leiper and John W. Burton. For a sum of $539, they purchased land from Thomas Robertson for a Confederate cemetery. This plot was located between the Shelbyville Pike and the N&C Railroad. Intentions were good, but money was very scarce following the war and the work languished, although from all over the South came inquiries seeking information about the last resting place of loved ones. In 1897, an old soldier wrote to the son of a comrade who had been killed at Murfreesboro saying that the grave had been marked with a plank and regretting he could not give more help because "I know you never looked on your father's manly face, you having been born after he entered the army." In 1888, the John Palmer Bivouac of the United Confederate Veterans purchased land in the new city cemetery as a resting place for the Confederate dead, with the old cemetery being sold to help pay for the relocation. This new plot in Evergreen Cemetery would be known as Confederate Circle. All known graves were exhumed and the remains moved to their present location. The process of memorialization of the Confederates by their direct survivors reached its climax in 1901 with the dedication of a statue on the courthouse square.[25]

Confederate Monument. *Courtesy of Bill Jakes.*

A FINAL FLURRY

The passing months of 1863 and 1864 continued to bring hard times to the people of Murfreesboro. One old man who traveled around the various army camps singing songs and entertaining the troops was found to have military information on his person, and he was shot "while trying to escape." The hand of the provost rested cruelly on the people. Every few days, expeditions were sent out to arrest citizens on suspicion of pro-Confederate activity. If the suspicions were strong enough, the troops were ordered to kill the suspects and to dispense with even the pretext of a trial.

Even after the danger of significant Confederate military action had passed, such actions continued. On January 7, 1865, the provost general for the area, Major General Robert Milroy, gave orders that farms listed in his attached order were to be visited and all livestock seized, all household furnishings loaded into wagons sent for the purpose (including taking the sashes out of the windows), the houses and all outbuildings burned and "the following persons…shot." The next paragraph orders that "the following will be hung to the first tree in front of their door and be allowed to hang there for an indefinite period. You will assure yourself they are dead before leaving." These death sentences applied to fifteen people. The instructions about hanging the men in their own yards imply that a hangman's noose was not to be used. Such a knot would cause death instantly, but these men were to be hanged with a simple slipknot so they would strangle to death slowly, in up to ten minutes. Being hanged in one's own yard would mean the man's wife and children would witness the death.[26] Similar orders went out as late in the war as May 1865 and document the execution without evidence or trial of over five hundred civilians.

Although the combat drew farther and farther away from Murfreesboro, the war remained a bitter reality. The prominent family of Judge Bromfield Ridley provides a prime example. The judge, an ardent secessionist, fled the county, leaving his wife to manage their plantation while their four sons served in the Confederate forces. A neighboring girl, fifteen-year-old F.E. Henderson, recorded in her diary for July 15, 1865: "The Yankees searched Mrs. Ridley's house for arms—found none." On July 20, she wrote, "Mrs. Judge Ridley's house was burned."[27]

And then it happened—first rumors and then definite news. The Army of Tennessee was moving north. Sherman might be on his way to the sea, but the Confederates were marching toward Tennessee. Soon, reports of fighting at Columbia reached the town, and then came the news of the bloodbath at Franklin. All this time the scattered U.S. garrisons from along the railroad were streaming into town to find refuge inside Fort Rosecrans.

W.H. King wrote in his memoir, "November 30, 1864—the Battle of Franklin—all my brothers came home except Brother Jim who was wounded and stayed with Billy Wilkerson, who also was wounded, at Mr. Jim Johnson's, five miles out on the Columbia Pike."[28] Another Murfreesboro resident, Emma Lane, wrote in her diary for December 5, "Can hear cannon firing in the direction of Nashville." On December 11 she noted, "Nearly all board fences have been torn down to make bunks for U.S. wounded."[29]

Upon reaching Nashville, the Confederate commander, John Bell Hood, divided his already weakened army by sending the infantry division commanded by William Brimage Bate to Murfreesboro to keep an eye on the nine thousand U.S. soldiers sheltering in Fort Rosecrans under the command of General Lovell Rousseau. Bedford Forrest was then ordered to take two divisions of cavalry, those of Buford and Jackson, and ride down the railroad, destroying the track as he went and then taking command at Murfreesboro. Forrest arrived on December 6.

On December 7, a U.S. force under Major General Robert Milroy, the harsh provost commander, sallied out from Fort Rosecrans to challenge Forrest. Forrest planned to oppose Milroy with his infantry under Bate and envelope the U.S. flanks with his cavalry, while his artillery commander, John Morton, swept into the Union rear, entering Murfreesboro from the east. The plan fell apart when Bate's infantry suddenly gave way.

William King described the event from the perspective of the townspeople:

> *Seven thousand Yankees went out on the Manson Pike and the Nashville Pike and made an attack on the Confederates, across the Pike from Cousin Mittie Gresham's home. Along where Jim Manson lived the Alabamians were stationed, and gave way, and the rest of the battle line was forced to fall back. General Forrest and the cavalry were between Harding's place and the Franklin road, waiting for the signal to charge into the rear of the Yankees and capture them. He surely was mad!*[30]

Although some skirmishing would continue in the vicinity for the next ten days, the issue was settled at Murfreesboro: the Rebs could not get in, and the Yanks could not get out. Forrest took advantage of the hospitality offered by the local people, especially those residents who had family in his command. His adjutant, Major Charles Anderson, was from the Murfreesboro area, and on December 9 he took Forrest to the home of his relatives, the Henderson family. Frances Elizabeth Henderson, fifteen years old, wrote in her diary, "Cold. Uncle Charlie went to camp but came back with General Forrest and spent the night. I had the honor of mending his pants."[31]

The Battle of Nashville, on December 15–16, was a decisive defeat for Hood's army, which fell back on the night of the sixteenth. Forrest moved his men away from Murfreesboro to become the rear guard of the retreat. King noted sadly:

> *A few days had been ours to enjoy and feed numbers of Confederate soldiers, to give them a dry place to lie down and sleep. Then off they returned South, hopeless and disheartened. Yet they were brave and endured to the end, feeling that all they had left was their honor as soldiers.*[32]

The war would drag on for almost five more months. Economic times would be harder than ever and the provost marshal would continue to rule with a stern, bloody hand, but the end of the conflict was near. As the weather warmed in April, news came that Robert E. Lee had surrendered the Army of Northern Virginia; the next month brought the news that Joseph Johnston had done the same with the remnants of the Army of Tennessee, and from Alabama came the news that Forrest had surrendered his command at Gainesville.

During the spring and into the early summer, the survivors of four years of war came home. But the home to which they returned was not the home they had left. Murfreesboro, the South and the United States had changed forever.

6
After the Storm

The end of the fighting did not end the problems faced by all the residents of Murfreesboro; indeed, new problems arose to replace the issues confronted during wartime. The first problem was to restore the structure of government. In 1861, officials had been elected under the auspices of the Confederate government; these men were ousted by the 1862 U.S. occupation and other officeholders elected under U.S. authority. These U.S. officials, in turn, were displaced by the return of the Confederates in late 1862, but following the Battle of Stones River, the town was considered a combat zone and was under martial law until the end of the war. The same was true for most of the state. Now, with the U.S. military preparing to withdraw, civil government structures had to be rebuilt from the ground up.

A second problem was restoring relations between the state and the U.S. government and creating a sense of loyalty to that restored relationship. Most Tennesseans did not want to be in the Union; their vote in June 1861 and their actions during the war made that quite clear. The force of arms might compel them to be part of the United States physically, but their hearts were not in the effort. Creating a sense of loyalty to the restored Union would be long-term work.

A third problem was defining the status of African Americans. The war had destroyed slavery, so black people were free, but free and what? Free and equal? Free and citizens? Free to survive as they might? The issue of citizenship would not be addressed for many months, until the Fourteenth and Fifteenth Amendments to the Constitution were written and adopted. Until then, the status of African Americans was in limbo.

Finally, there was the economy. The South was devastated and destitute. It did not matter if a person had been pro-Confederate or pro-Union, free or slave; they all faced the same desperate postwar devastation. Of the generation of males who had fought for the Confederacy, 50 percent were either dead or permanently crippled. Able-bodied men to do the work of rebuilding were not to be had in sufficient numbers. The term "Reconstruction" is a misnomer; very little aid was forthcoming to reconstruct anything. So the problems were unsolved, and the issues festered.

The census of 1860 shows that Rutherford County, of which Murfreesboro is the county seat, had 10,308 horses, 4,348 mules and asses, 6,249 milk cows, 23,133 sheep and 64,877 hogs, with a total value of $2,115,432. By 1870, the taking of the next census, all these totals were down 20 percent, with the value of all livestock only $595,493. The value of real estate had suffered an equally disastrous decline. In 1860, the total value of the county's real estate was $15,759,758, but in 1870, it was $6,020,575. Personal property had suffered most of all, declining from $17,835,603 in 1860 to $1,055,297 in 1870. Many families had left the area looking for better economic opportunities.[1]

John Spence described the town:

> *The government offices are busied collecting and selling all articles in their use, from saw mills, down to a horse nail at auction. Things thus sold was knocked of at a great sacrifice to the bidder. Those having money to invest in this way was likely to make it profitable.*
>
> *We now take a view of the town as it appeared. Murfreesboro was held as a military point during the war. By the close things was in a confused condition. The best houses were used and much abused by the military power during their stay. Numbers of houses were either burned or pulled down, they said to make field hospitals, but never made. This was done to destroy and to annoy the people.*
>
> *The brick wall around the court yard pulled down. The jail house burned which had been a quartering of negros, it having been vacant some time as prison. The market house on the north side of the public square had disappeared. The business rooms on the public square were used for commissary stores. There was a hospital established in the three store rooms on the north east corner of the public square, the counters and shelving taken out. Fences round dwelling lots near all*

destroyed. Scarcely a whole fence to be seen in town. Wagons passing all directions over lots and gardens.[2]

The period immediately following the close of the war became known to many as the "barefoot time." Stone bruises and foot afflictions were quite prevalent, as

no covering for the feet was worn from about the first of April until the ground froze hard in the fall. The men usually possessed one suit of clothes for every day of the year, and they wore that suit on every day of the year, and often for two or three years, both daily and Sunday too. The woman who was fortunate enough to own a "bombazine," relict of prewar days, would array herself in it on special occasions and pose as a grand dame.[3]

For Murfreesboro, as for the rest of Tennessee, Reconstruction ended in 1869 with the election of DeWitt Clinton Senter as governor. Senter convinced the state legislature that the prohibition against allowing former Confederates to vote should be ended. This action filled the voting rolls with a majority who favored a more conservative approach to government and a return to something resembling the social relations that had existed prior to the war. This did not mean disenfranchisement of all African Americans; neither did it mean de jure "Jim Crow" segregation; those things did not become features of life for another generation. It did mean there would be no social revolution in matters of race relations. It also meant the Ku Klux Klan disappeared in Tennessee in 1869, since the goals of maintaining the social status quo antebellum could be achieved at the ballot box.

Today, the Civil War is not forgotten in Murfreesboro. The courthouse, which was the focal point of Forrest's Birthday Raid in 1862, is still the focus of downtown and the locus of county government. Oaklands, where the 9th Michigan fought the Texas Rangers, still stands and is open to the public. On the edge of town, the ordered rows of graves in the National Cemetery are a reminder of the cost in blood of preserving the Union, while Confederate Circle in the city burying ground is a hallowed memorial to those who fell defending their homes. For many residents, Stones River National Battlefield is simply open green space for a jog or a place to walk their dogs, but to those with a mind attuned to the meaning of the past, it is hallowed ground where the fate of this nation once hung by a thread.

Old wounds heal slowly and faint scars still remain. The Civil War will always be part of the heritage of Murfreesboro.

Famous Civil War Figures from Murfreesboro

R utherford County, based on population, is said to have furnished more men to the Confederate cause than any other county in the state. At least six men born in Rutherford County rose to the rank of brigadier general either before or after the war, including William Barksdale, Henry Eustace McCulloch, Ben McCulloch, Winfield Scott Featherston, Thomas Benton Smith and Joseph Palmer. Of these, Palmer would be the only one to make his lifelong home in Rutherford County.

The American Civil War, or the War Between the States, was a defining time in our nation's history. Lives were forever changed as a result of a nation at war with itself, and virtually no man, woman or child—black or white, young or old—was left unscathed. Sadly, many stories have been lost to history, so the brief biographical sketches included herein merely provide a glimpse into the lives of some who survived the war and some who did not. Emotions ran high, fortunes and loved ones were lost and the world changed. The war was a family affair—families united in their struggle against an enemy, and families were torn apart due to differing opinions. Murfreesboro, after all, was a town captured, and 150 years later, it has yet to surrender.

SAM DAVIS

Mother, do not grieve for me…I do not hate to Die.

These immortal words of young Sam Davis were ones that no mother, then or now, would ever want to hear. Yet these very words were written from his jail cell in Pulaski in a note to his mother on November 26, 1863, before he was to be hanged the next day:

> *Dear Mother,*
> *O, how painful it is to write you! I have got to die tomorrow morning—to be hanged by the Federals. Mother, do not grieve for me. I must bid you good-bye for evermore. Mother I do not hate to die. Give my love to all.*
> *Your son,*
> *Sam*[1]

But Sam's story didn't end that fateful morning of November 27; by the end of the century, Sam Davis would become larger in death than he had been during his brief time on earth. As he passed from life into legend, he became a martyr, not only to the Confederate cause for which he chose to give his all, but also to the terrible waste of more than 620,000 mothers' sons as well.

Sam Davis was born on a farm near Smyrna, Tennessee, on October 6, 1842, the oldest of eight children born to Charles Louis and Jane Simmons Davis. By 1860, Charles was the fourth-largest taxpayer in Rutherford County, owning more than eight hundred acres of land.

A good education was essential to the Davis family, and Sam attended a nearby school until he was seventeen. One of his teachers recalled that he was about

> *five feet and nine or ten inches, with splendid physical proportion, and symmetrical features. He was modest and unassuming in demeanor, quiet and deferential, never domineering. There was an indefinable reserve force about him that challenged both respect and esteem of others, and he soon became a leader among his schoolmates.*[2]

In November 1860, when Sam was eighteen, he enrolled in the Western Military Institute in Nashville. In the spring of 1861, he left school and, in April, joined his hometown company, the Rutherford

Rifles, under the command of Captain William Ledbetter. This would become Company I, 1st Regiment, Tennessee Volunteer Infantry. The regiment served briefly in Virginia but was in Tennessee for the Battle of Shiloh, where Sam was wounded. In October, it was at Perryville, and Sam was wounded again. Then the regiment went back to Murfreesboro for the Battle of Stones River on December 31. Following this battle, Major General Benjamin Cheatham authorized a unit of scouts under the command of Captain Henry Shaw to be the eyes and ears of the army and thus supply him with much-needed information. Sam was detached from his regiment by orders of General Braxton Bragg for service with the Coleman Scouts. John, Sam's older half brother, was also serving with the Coleman Scouts; the majority of scouts were from the Middle Tennessee area and knew it well. The main mission of the Coleman Scouts would be to pick up information from various post offices; deliver it to Shaw's headquarters near Columbia, where he would then rewrite it in cipher and sign off as E. Coleman, his alias; and then carry the information to Bragg's headquarters near Chattanooga.

The Coleman Scouts provided valuable and accurate information to General Bragg, and their efforts contributed to the Confederate victory at Chickamauga in September 1863. By early November, with Federal forces approaching, Bragg again turned to these brave men to obtain additional information. Sam left for his last mission on November 10, 1863. He first went to see the lovely Mary Kate Patterson on November 14 at her home near Nashville. His next stop was a visit with his family in Smyrna. Little did they know that this would be the last time they would see him alive.

By November 19, Sam had met with Captain Shaw and was given information concerning Union troop movements, maps and descriptions of Federal fortifications and eleven Louisville and Cincinnati newspapers with more pertinent details. This important package, along with mail and the articles smuggled out of Nashville, was entrusted to Sam, and he began his second leg of the journey south toward Chattanooga and General Bragg. The next day, November 20, 1863, in Giles County near Minor Hill, not far from the Alabama state line, Sam stopped to rest before crossing the Tennessee River. He was approached by two men in what appeared to be Confederate uniforms who ordered him to halt. One of the men told Sam that he was conscripting him into the Confederate army, but Sam, being in uniform, explained that he was already a member of the 1st Tennessee and provided the pass given to him by Captain Shaw and signed by authority of General Bragg. It read, "By order of General Bragg, Samuel Davis has permission to pass on scouting duty anywhere in Middle Tennessee or north of the Tennessee River he may think proper."[3] The two men insisted on taking Sam before their commanding officer and demanded his sidearms, as well as the pouches filled with maps, letters, newspapers and dispatches. Sam quickly realized he was being taken prisoner and attempted to escape, but to no avail.

Sam was delivered to Captain L.H. Naron from Mississippi, also known as "Captain Chickasaw," General Dodge's chief of scouts. After seeing the information that Sam was carrying, Captain Chickasaw immediately took him to Pulaski, where he was brought before General Dodge. Amazed at the accuracy of the maps and information, and desperate to discover the identity of E. Coleman, General Dodge offered Sam leniency for his cooperation. He later said of this meeting:

> *Davis met me modestly. He was a fine, soldierly-looking young fellow. He had a frank, open face and was bright. I tried to impress upon him the danger he was in, and told him that I knew he was only a messenger, and urged him, on the promise of lenient treatment, to divulge the source of all the information.*

Davis replied, "I won't tell sir."[4] General Dodge then ordered Sam sent to the provost marshal, where he was placed in a cell and told that he would be sentenced to death as a spy if he did not cooperate.

Sam was court-martialed on November 24 at 2:00 p.m.; he was found guilty of being a spy and sentenced to death by hanging. On Friday, November 27, 1863, at 10:00 a.m., his death sentence was carried out. As he took his seat on the wagon loaded with a plain pine coffin and headed for the gallows, he asked Captain Armstrong about the Battle at Missionary Ridge and was told of Bragg's defeat. As he climbed the steps to the scaffold, Captain Chickasaw rode up with a repeat of General Dodge's offer. Sam was told one final time that if he would only tell General Dodge who had given him the information, he would be provided with his horse, sidearms and an escort to Confederate lines. When Sam did not answer, General Chickasaw again pleaded with him to save his own life. It was then that Sam looked Chickasaw straight in the eye and unknowingly uttered his own epitaph: "If I had a thousand lives to live, I would rather give them all than betray a friend."[5]

Sam turned and took his place, and the trap was sprung. At age twenty-one, Samuel Davis passed from life into legend. Several days later, family members came to Pulaski to claim Sam's remains, which were then transported to his home near Smyrna, where he was buried in the family cemetery.

WILLIAM LEDBETTER JR.
AND THE RUTHERFORD RIFLES

William Ledbetter Jr. was born on April 21, 1831, the son of William Ledbetter Sr. and Eliza Welborn Ledbetter. William Jr. grew up enjoying the advantages of an affluent family lifestyle and attended Union University prior to the Civil War. On May 6, 1857, he and Mary Catherine Lytle were married.

In early 1861, when all of the unrest and talk of secession began in Rutherford County, both William Ledbetter Jr. and Sr. were among the leaders of the secessionist movement. William Sr. was granted a $7,500 advance by the Tennessee legislature to build an armory in Murfreesboro, crafting Harpers Ferry rifles for the Army of Tennessee. Somewhere between 240 and 480 of these rifles were produced by the Ledbetter Armory during the war.[1]

On April 23, 1861, a group of men gathered at the Rutherford County Courthouse intent on organizing a military company. All of the men were of good character, and many were descendants of the earliest settlers of the area. They would come to be known as the Rutherford Rifles, which would become Company I, 1st Tennessee Infantry Regiment, with William Ledbetter Jr. serving as its captain. Many of the names of men who were part of this company then, in addition to Ledbetter, are very familiar to present-day Rutherford County: Anderson, Avent, Bass, Batey, Becton, Beesley, Blair, Brothers, Butler, Carney, Cates, Crichlow, Crockett, Davis, Hall, Halliburton, Haynes, Holloway, James, Jarrett, Jetton, Jenkins, King, McFarlin, Miller, Mitchell, Morton, Murfree, Ransom, Rucker, etc.

And some were not from Rutherford County:

There were four Germans in Company I, Ledbetter's, all of whom made valiant soldiers and splendid citizens of Murfreesboro after the war. They were: Fred Crass, who came here in 1856, Adam Bock and George Walter and a young German named Loeb, all of whom came here a short time after the arrival of Crass.[2]

The men spent about a week in daily drills before departing the Murfreesboro Depot on May 2, 1861, when hundreds of citizens turned out for a farewell parade. They arrived in Nashville at eleven o'clock that morning and marched around the square to the tune of "Annie Laurie."[3] July would find them training at Camp Cheatham. They were mustered into Confederate service on August 1, 1861, and would prove themselves to be one of the most outstanding companies from the county, seeing action at Shiloh, Murfreesboro, Chickamauga, Kennesaw Mountain, the Atlanta Campaign and in Hood's invasion to retake Tennessee. Alfred Horsley of Columbia, Tennessee, had this to say of the Rutherford Rifles:

The Butlers of our regiment were fine soldiers. Jack, captain of the Railroad Company, and Joe, his brother, lieutenant, refined and handsome as a woman, but brave as Caesar, literally shot to pieces at Perryville, Doc [William Ledbetter Jr.] in stature like a Roman gladiator, shot at Missionary Ridge. For years we had seen his grand Apollo-like form in the front of the Rutherford Rifles, rendered more majestic by comparison with the diminutive form of captain "Doc" Ledbetter. No matter how dark the night or how long the march, when the "imminent perilous edge of battle" was in sight, the Rutherford Rifles always had a long battle line and "Doc" Ledbetter was at the head. I often recall him and his company, as they appeared before battle. I think…the Rutherford Rifles was the best company in the 1ˢᵗ Tennessee Regiment. Sam Davis who died at Pulaski rather than betray a confidence was a member of the Rutherford Rifles… If all the men in the Southern army had been like the Rutherford Rifles, we could have camped on the shores of Lake Erie instead of the Chattahoochie. My memory is a picture gallery in which is seen this splendid company of man at the moment of battle—all others looking like skeletons, but the Rutherford company of men, a long line of tall, majestic men. Caesar would have placed them in his "Tenth Legion" or Napoleon in his "Old Guard." The Ransoms, the Wades, the Kings, the Bezles (Beazles), the Jarrats were all grand men, but like Saul, "Doc" Ledbetter rose proudly preeminent above them all, and poor Hardy Murfree, the best of men, his memory is worthy to be honored with the tears of all good and brave men. All honor to Rutherford County.[4]

Spencer Akin, general agent with the Nashville, Chattanooga & St. Louis Railway, wrote a letter to family members and said the following of Captain Ledbetter: "He was a glorious man in a glorious cause, a true soldier and an honest gentleman, a steady comrade and friend."[5] Captain Ledbetter said of himself that "he was the oldest captain in the First Tennessee Volunteers [he was thirty years old at the time of his enlistment], he was the smallest in stature [five feet, six inches tall] and had the largest company in the regiment, and more men than any other company that were over six feet tall."[6]

Captain Ledbetter would lead his men ably and nobly throughout the war, suffering wounds first at Atlanta on July 22, while leading his company in the charge on Union earthworks south of Bald Hill, and then again just four months later at the ill-fated Battle of Franklin. He was captured by Union forces on December 3, 1864, near Versailles, Kentucky, and the next month, January 1865, would escape while en route from Louisville, Kentucky, to a Fort Delaware Federal prison.[7] "He escaped by jumping from a rail car into an icy river, recuperated with locals who protected and nursed him to health, and rejoined the Confederates, only to surrender May 4, 1865 in Athens, Ga."[8] There were approximately 150 young men in the Rutherford Rifles who went to war in 1861, and four years later, of those from Murfreesboro, only eleven would return home.

Upon his return home, Captain Ledbetter found that his father had died during his absence, and his house, which was located on the Salem Pike (Highway 99) and is still standing today, was confiscated by Yankees to be later auctioned in bankruptcy. Sadly, "the family was forced to live in an un-partitioned room above the Planters Union Bank on the Murfreesboro square, hanging sheets to provide some semblance of privacy."[9] This was the same bank where his father had served as president before the war.

Ledbetter turned his life to public service after the war, serving as city alderman from 1871 to 1875 and city treasurer from 1874 to 1875. He died on July 15, 1906, and is buried in Evergreen Cemetery.

JOSEPH PALMER

While Rutherford County can boast of having five men born in the county who would earn the rank of brigadier general either before or during the Civil War, there was only one who would make Murfreesboro his lifelong home. Joseph B. Palmer was the only general to serve in the Confederate army who was living in the county at the beginning of the war. He fought in two battles for his hometown and was one of the most frequently wounded generals on either side, being wounded six different times in battle. When the war ended, Joseph Palmer was commanding all of the Tennesseans still with the main Confederate army and was one of the few generals who took all of his men back to their home state. Characteristically, no general of the Civil War better represented his native state than did General Joseph B. Palmer of Tennessee. It was said of him by his peers that "he was a man of ability, of courage and of convictions. His whole life was clean and admirable.[1]

Joseph Benjamin Palmer was born on November 1, 1825, the son of William and Mildred Johns Palmer, in the Walter Hill area near the Stones River. After his parents separated, and following his mother's death in 1831, young Joseph was reared by his maternal grandparents, Joseph and Elizabeth Johns. On January 1, 1844, nineteen-year-old Joseph enrolled in Union University. After attending school there for two years, finances did not permit his continuing until graduation; he was, however, accepted into the law office of Hardy Murfree Burton, where he studied law until he was admitted to the Rutherford County legal bar in 1848. He was able to open his own office when he was only twenty-two years old and was known to be a good lawyer. He became interested in politics and was soon a leader of the Whig Party. At age twenty-four, he was elected to represent his district in the Tennessee General Assembly. At age twenty-eight, on February 14, 1854, Joseph married Ophelia Maria Burrus, later described in *Prominent Tennesseans* as "one of the most beautiful women that Tennessee ever produced."[2] Sadly, their marriage lasted less than two and a half years before her untimely death. Their only son, Horace, was less than a year old, and his grief-stricken father would remain a widower for the next thirteen years. A year before his wife's death and no longer a state legislator, Joseph had been elected mayor of Murfreesboro and served four consecutive years, from 1855 to 1859. The 1860 census shows Joseph Palmer, lawyer, living with his four-year-old son, nine slaves and a personal estate valued at $14,000, with real estate appraised at $1,200; thus, Joseph Palmer was a fairly wealthy man.[3]

Although pro-Union and strongly opposed to secession initially, Joseph Palmer chose loyalty to his state when the war came and, in so doing, turned his back on a very successful law practice and comfortable lifestyle, including parenting of his young son. In April 1861, Joseph began his military career with the organization of Company C, 18th Tennessee Infantry, and on May 20, 1861, was commissioned captain. On June

11, 1861, the 18th Tennessee Volunteer Infantry Regiment was officially organized. Captain Palmer was elected unanimously as its commander and commissioned as Colonel Joseph B. Palmer, a rank he would retain for nearly three and a half years.[4] Palmer was well liked and quite respected by his men, and despite his lack of formal military training, the 18th Tennessee Infantry became an outstanding fighting unit. After the war, General Palmer wrote a condensed history of the regiment and, in his own words, stated

> *that the regiment was organized on the 11th of June, 1861, at Camp Trousdale, this state, by the election of Palmer as colonel. It consisted of ten companies and among the captains were: M.R. Rushing, W.R. Butler, B.F. Webb, B.G. Wood, all of this county. The first battle in which the regiment participated was at Fort Donelson, which, after hard and stubborn fighting and much suffering, surrendered to the Federal forces on February 16, 1862.*
>
> *Col. Palmer and his field officers were imprisoned at Fort Warren, Boston Harbor. All of the officers and men were exchanged in September, 1862. The regiment was organized, when Palmer was again elected colonel, and W.R. Butler, lieutenant colonel. This regiment was attached to the command of General John C. Brown.*
>
> *After Colonel Palmer was breveted to the rank of brigadier-general, it was known as Palmer's Brigade. It was surrendered at Goldsboro, North Carolina on May 2, 1865. At the battle of Murfreesboro General Palmer was wounded three times, in the famous but devastating Breckinridge's Charge, once by a Minié ball through the calf of the leg, once through the shoulder and a shell wound on the knee. But he did not leave the field till the close of the engagement, and then brought off his regiment in good order.[5]*

The Battle of Stones River, from December 31, 1862, to January 2, 1863, was devastating to both Palmer and his men. Palmer's Brigade suffered 425 casualties over the three days of fighting. The 18th Tennessee reported 19 killed, 108 wounded and 8 missing, the majority of which occurred on January 2. This totals 135 casualties of the 430 fit for duty at the time, a casualty rate of more than 31 percent.[6] Bragg's army began its sad retreat from Murfreesboro on January 4, 1863, leaving the wounded Palmer "in the neighborhood of Allisonia"[7] and his hometown in the hands of the enemy for the duration of the war.

Following his recovery from wounds received at Murfreesboro, Palmer would rejoin his men in time for the Battle of Chickamauga on September 19, where he would again be severely wounded, once again in his right shoulder. This left him temporarily unfit for active field duty, and he was appointed to district command in the Department of Tennessee on November 18, 1863. He resumed brigade command on June 27, 1864, in the Army of Tennessee and participated in the Atlanta Campaign. Palmer fought during the Battle of Jonesborough and was wounded on September 1, 1864. Following a lengthy and painful recovery, he once again rejoined the field of battle and was commissioned a brigadier general on November 15, 1864.[8] Palmer fought in the Battle of Franklin on November 30 and then the Battle of Nashville on December 15–16. He was part of the army's rear guard during the retreat from Nashville, after which what remained of the pitiful Tennessee regiments of the Army of Tennessee were consolidated and placed under Palmer's command. He would lead them on through the 1865 Carolinas Campaign. Palmer participated in the Battle of Bentonville and was once again wounded but stayed in command until April 26, 1865, surrendering on May 1 along with General Joseph E. Johnston. He was paroled from Greensboro, North Carolina.[9]

Palmer returned to Murfreesboro and resumed his law practice. He married Mrs. Margaret Mason, a widow he had met during the war, on June 10, 1869, and they would make their home on East Main Street in a fine new brick home. Joseph Palmer died on November 4, 1890, and is buried in Evergreen Cemetery.

MARY KATE PATTERSON

Spying wasn't just for the boys. It was dangerous business for everyone involved—male or female—and the punishment for anyone caught could be imprisonment or worse, such as banishment or hanging. The American Civil War was the first war in which women could take such an active role without the fear of losing their status as "ladies," and they were involved in just about every aspect of the war effort. Without a voice and without a vote, ladies made their presence known, proving their worth alongside their male counterparts in ways never before imagined. It was quickly recognized that there was a lot more beneath their bonnets than just a bunch of pretty curls.

Famous Civil War Figures from Murfreesboro

Mary Kate Patterson was born on October 15, 1844, in Warren County, Kentucky. She was the daughter of Dr. Hugh Patterson and his wife, Eleanora. The family moved to Tennessee about 1850 and actually lived in Davidson County on Nolensville Road in a community known as Rashboro. The area was so near the Rutherford County line that when the LaVergne Post Office was established in 1857, it would be the one to handle their mail. Kate's ties to Rutherford County would go far beyond mail delivery.

As a young girl, Mary Kate was described as being "vivacious...with flashing brown eyes and bouncy dark brown curls."[1] As with so many other young people of the 1850s, her education was interrupted by the Civil War.

During the war, Mary Kate's brother, Everard Meade Patterson, served with the Coleman Scouts, and it was through this association that she would meet her future husband, John G. Davis, brother of Sam.

Since Mary Kate's father was a doctor, he was able to obtain needed medical supplies for the Confederacy. Mary Kate and her cousin Robbie Woodruff made frequent trips to Nashville and, wearing voluminous riding habits, were able to conceal large quantities of the drugs. She also had a special built buggy with a false bottom:

In the large seat of my buggy I would often bring out cavalry saddles, bridles, boots, spurs, gray cloth, and I smuggled medicines such as quinine, morphine, etc. I have brought $500 and $600 worth of medicine out at one time around my waist. Quinine and morphine were very high.[2]

Mary Kate used her charm and beauty in obtaining information, newspapers and medical supplies from Union soldiers in Nashville. She felt that it was imperative to maintain good relations with the Federal officer in charge—"I always keep on the good side of the Commanding General and could get passes when I desired to do so"[3]—thus allowing her to pass through Yankee lines at just about any time. She once stated, "I went to Nashville very often so I always kept posted; had many confidential friends there, always ready to help me when asked."[4]

It was during one of the Coleman Scouts rendezvous at the Patterson home that Mary Kate met and fell in love with John Davis, older half brother of Sam Davis. She and John were eventually married on February 25, 1864. Kate developed a warm friendship with Sam and even had a pair of fine boots made for him in Nashville, never dreaming that these boots would walk him up the gallows to his death.

On the night of November 14, 1863, Sam tossed a pebble against a window of the Patterson home and told Mary Kate that he would be spending the next few days in "Rains Thicket." He gave her a list of much-needed supplies he wanted her to acquire in Nashville for General Bragg. He asked her to bring breakfast and horse feed to him the next morning and requested that Robbie Woodruff come along as well and spend the day.

> We found him up, looking as bright as if he had slept all night, and, oh, he did enjoy his good warm breakfast, for we rode fast and had his coffee in a jug to keep it warm. Two of my little brothers brought our dinner and we spent a nice, pleasant Sunday together—the last he spent on earth but one.[5]

On Monday, Mary Kate and Robbie went to Nashville on their "shopping" expedition and brought Sam the items she had procured, including three "wash balls" of soap, a tooth brush, Louisville and Cincinnati newspapers and a notebook in his possession when captured.

When the Davis family received news that a young soldier bearing a strong likeness to Sam had been hanged as a spy, the family feared the worst. John Davis was quite sick with typhoid fever, and the ever-loyal friend of the family, the fearless Mary Kate, was appointed the task of determining if this was their son. In her typical heroic and courageous manner, Mary Kate went to Major General L. Harrison Rousseau, requesting a pass to immediately go to Pulaski to be near the bedside of a dear aunt who was dying. Although advised to wait until morning, Mary Kate and her cousin, nine-year-old Willie Woodruff, set out immediately. While in Pulaski, Mary Kate and Willie stayed in the home of a Dr. Batts and his family, which ironically overlooked the very gallows where Sam Davis was hanged. It was this sad news that Kate brought back to the Davis family, and a few days later, John Kennedy and Sam's youngest brother, Oscar, returned to Pulaski to claim Sam's body.

This was not the last tragedy that would test Kate's strength. Just a little over four years later, on February 27, 1867, her beloved husband, John Davis, was killed in a steamboat explosion, along with Captain Shaw. Kate would wed two more times, next to a Mr. Hill, who died young, and the third time, on December 30, 1884, to a former Confederate soldier,

Colonel Robert Kyle, of Texas. They made their home in Rutherford County near LaVergne.

Mary Kate Patterson died on July 6, 1931, at the age of ninety-three. Her dedication to the South and to the Confederacy never diminished. She visited Confederate veterans in rest homes and made monetary contributions far beyond what she could afford. She was the first woman to be buried in Confederate Circle at Mount Olivet Cemetery in Nashville.

BROMFIELD RIDLEY JR.

Bromfield Ridley Jr. was born on January 31, 1845, at Fairmont, the plantation home of his parents, Bromfield Lewis Ridley Sr. and Rebecca Thompson Crosthwaite Ridley, located in the Old Jefferson community of Rutherford County. Like so many other young men of the day, Bromfield Jr. attended the Nashville Military Institute prior to the Civil War.

At the time of the Battle of Stones River, Bromfield was a mere lad of seventeen and saw himself

as one of what was known as the "Seed Corn of the South," too young to be called on for service, the limit being eighteen. I would go along with the soldier boys "bearded like the pard, jealous in honor, seeking bubble reputation at the cannon's mouth," and join in the revelry—raids in progress about the State insane asylum, dashes on the chicken road, also about Nolensville, the Hermitage, around Nashville, Lebanon, Gallatin, and other places.[1]

It was during the Battle of Stones River, on one of these such "outings," that he and four or five other boys, not members of any command, engaged in "picking up" some 212 Federal stragglers and turned them over to the Confederate pickets at Black's Shop:

I had brothers in Morgan's cavalry, stationed at Black's shop, the intersection of the Murfreesboro and Lebanon and Jefferson and Milton pikes, and a brother in Bragg's army, and my father's home was, of course, the rendezvous of many on our side. Wharton's cavalry was near Triune, in front of Hardee. Wheeler was below Lavergne, while John Morgan was at Black's shop watching approaches from Lebanon.[2]

When Bromfield compiled his journal with his thoughts of the battle and, in particular, the day of Breckinridge's charge at McFadden's Ford, he would remember his mother's concern for her husband and sons:

> *About three o'clock on Friday the firing of artillery and small arms was more terrific than usual. A fearful battle was evidently in progress. It turned out to be Breckinridge's fatal charge…that he was driving one or two lines into the river…when fifty-two pieces of artillery opened up and almost decimated his ranks. On that Friday, my dear mother made her way to Murfreesboro through the Confederate pickets to look after husband and sons, and reached there, after passing through long lines of cavalry mounted, and ready for the conflict.[3]*

Bromfield obviously had great admiration for the "Thunderbolt of the Confederacy" when he wrote:

> *On December 8, 1862…we received the news that General John Morgan had taken his own command and Hanson's Kentucky brigade and captured 2,000 prisoners at Hartsville. Morgan returned a lion, and my young heart leaped with joy when I went up to Black's shop and saw the 2,000 blue coats filing by. Every tongue was in his praise, and the Confederate congress congratulated the brilliant achievement.[4]*

It was not surprising that Bromfield would join up with Company F, Ward's Regiment, Morgan's Cavalry, and follow the regiment through the Battles of Milton; Carthage; Lancaster, Kentucky; Snow Hill; Grassy Creek, Kentucky; and McMinnville. Then, in July 1863, when the Confederate army was encamped at Tullahoma, young Ridley was ordered to report to Major General A.P. Stewart as an aide de camp. He would remain with Stewart throughout all of the campaigns under the general's command until the end of the war. Stewart would later say of him, "He served with me, very creditably, to the end of the war, or 'the surrender' as it is usually termed."[5]

After the war, Ridley returned home and attended Cumberland University School of Law in Lebanon. Following graduation, he made his home in Murfreesboro, where he was a junior partner in the law firm with his father. He served as Murfreesboro city alderman from 1878 to 1881 and then, on December 4, 1879, married Idelette DeBur Lyon. In 1892, Bromfield Ridley was one of three innovative citizens who established the Murfreesboro Street Railway. Unfortunately, the company, consisting of eight cars, twenty-four mules, terminal barns and three miles of track, lasted only about a year. Ridley believed in the recovery of the postwar years and in the future of Murfreesboro and was not intimidated by the failure of the streetcar venture. That same year, he and his two business partners started the Murfreesboro Water Works and, sometime later, began laying sewer lines within the city.

In 1906, Ridley published *Battles and Sketches of the Army of Tennessee*, and he would say of his writing, "The journal is that of a boy, and the sketches where written by the author are as impressions made upon a boy."[6] He continued to practice law in Murfreesboro until his death on January 12, 1917. He is buried in Evergreen Cemetery.

Notes

CHAPTER 1

1. Rutherford County Historical Society (RCHS) Collection, Box 1, Folder 12.
2. Joe Hatcher, "No Votes for Lincoln," clipping in Womack Collection, Box 16, Folder 140.
3. *Murfreesboro News*, September 26, 1860; October 17, 1860, microfilm, Linebaugh Public Library, Murfreesboro.
4. James Moore King Collection, Box 7, Folder 14, Albert Gore Research Center, Middle Tennessee State University.
5. James Moore King, "Colonel James Moore King: A Southern Gentleman, 1792–1877," typescript, James Moore King Collection, series 3, Albert Gore Research Center.
6. James Moore King Collection.
7. Mike West, "Stones River: Palmer's Life Illustrates Tennessee's Plight," *Murfreesboro Post*, July 3, 2011.
8. Hatcher, "No Votes for Lincoln."
9. *Murfreesboro News*, microfilm, Linebaugh Public Library, November 28, 1860.
10. *Rutherford Telegraph*, publications of Rutherford County Historical Society, vol. 39.
11. Hatcher, "No Votes for Lincoln."

12. Ibid.

13. John C. Spence, *Annals of Rutherford County*, vol. 11, 1829–1870; *Publications of the Rutherford County Historical Society*, vol. 39, p. 152.

14. Neff, *Tennessee's Battered Brigadier*, 24.

15. *Murfreesboro Post*, "Rutherford Rifles Fire True," July 17, 2011.

16. Ibid.

17. G.W. Wharton to Daniel Weeden, Womach Collection, Box 17, Folder 213.

18. Moses Joseph Nichols to Malinda Jared, July 1, 1861, in *Tennessee Civil War Source Book*, tennesseecivilwarsourcebook.com.

19. John Bradford to his sister, July 2, 1861, in *Tennessee Civil War Source Book*.

20. James E. Taft to James Caldwell, July 10, 1861, in *Tennessee Civil War Source Book*.

21. Edward Bradford to his mother, July 12, 1861, in *Tennessee Civil War Source Book*.

22. Edward Bradford to his father, May 30, 1861, in *Tennessee Civil War Source Book*; Allen, *Winds of Change*, 14.

23. Wilson et al., *Letters to Laura*, 35.

24. John Bradford to his father, July 19, 1861, in *Tennessee Civil War Source Book*; "Report on the Strength of the Provisional Army of Tennessee," July 31, 1861, in *Tennessee Civil War Source Book*.

25. James Moore King Collection, Undated, Box 1, Folder 1.

26. Kate Carney Diary, June 9, 1861, docsouth.unc.edu; *Publications of the Rutherford County Historical Society*, vol. 39, p. 1.

27. Spence, *Annals of Rutherford County*, 154.

CHAPTER 2

1. Spence, *Diary*, 12–13.

2. Ready, *Journal*, February 11, 1862.

3. Wilson et al., *Letters to Laura*, 76–77.

4. Spence, *Diary*, 16–18.

5. *Official Records of the War of the Rebellion*, ser. 1, vol. 7, 889 (hereafter cited as *OR*).

6. Ibid., vol. 7, 905.

7. Ibid., 912.

8. Duke, *History of Morgan's Cavalry*, 69–81, describes several of these incidents.

9. Neff and Pollitz, *Bride and the Bandit*, 160; Ready, *Journal*, March 3, 1862; Spence, *Diary*, 18.
10. Narcissa Hall to Andrew Johnson, June 27, 1862, in *Tennessee Civil War Source Book.*
11. Ready, *Journal*, March 5, 1862.
12. Ibid.
13. Jones, *Un-Civil War*, 2–3, contains the Spence citation.
14. McHenry, *Webster's American Military Biographies*, 285–86.
15. Spence, *Diary*, March 15, 1862, in *Tennessee Civil War Source Book.*
16 Bradley, *With Blood and Fire*, vi.
17. Henderson, *Story of Murfreesboro*, 168.
18. Jones, *Un-Civil War*, 4; RCHS, Box 1, Folder 7, Albert Gore Research Center.
19. William Mark Eames Papers, March 20, 1862, in *Tennessee Civil War Source Book.*
20. Beatty, *Citizen Soldier*, 122–23.
21. Spence, *Diary*, April 1, 1862, in *Tennessee Civil War Source Book.* Bradley, *With Blood and Fire*, 52–53, gives an example of reparations on behalf of U.S. soldiers killed by guerrillas.
22. Ready, *Journal*, April 20, 1862.
23. Jones, *Un-Civil War*, 20.
24. William H. King Memoirs, typescript, James Moore King Collection, Albert Gore Research Center.
25. Andrew Johnson to Colonel Parkhurst, May 11, 1862, in *Tennessee Civil War Source Book.*
26. *Union Volunteer*, May 30, 1862, microfilm, Linebaugh Public Library, History Collection. This paper was published under the auspices of the U.S. occupation forces. Captain Charles V. DeLand was the editor.
27. Bergeron, *Papers of Andrew Johnson*, vol. 5, 410–11.
28. Carney, *Diary*, June 1, 1862, docsouth.unc.edu.
29. *Nashville Daily Union*, July 9, 1862, Tennessee State Library and Archives.

CHAPTER 3

1. Carney, *Diary*, July 12, 1862; *OR*, ser. 1, vol. 16, pt. 1, 794.
2. Jordan and Pryor, *Campaigns*, 175; Iven Diary, July 13, 1862.
3. Jordan and Pryor, *Campaigns*, 160–61.
4. Ibid., 163 fn.

5. Belt and Nichols, *Onward Southern Soldiers*, 83.
6. Henderson, *Story of Murfreesboro*, 84.
7. Hughes, *Hearthstones*.
8. Iven *Diary*, July 13, 1862; Carney, *Diary*, July 13, 1862. The two accounts agree in general but differ in detail.
9. Spence, *Diary*, 48.
10. Poole, *Cracker Cavaliers*, 22–23.
11. Wyeth, *That Devil Forrest*, 78–79.
12. Pittard Collection, Miscellaneous Papers, Civil War Sites, Box 1, Folder 7.
13. Spence, *Diary*, 49; *OR*, ser. 1, vol. 16, pt. 1, 805.
14. Iven, *Diary*, July 13, 1862.
15. Carney, *Diary*, July 13, 1862.
16. William M. Eames to his wife, July 14, 1862; *Publications of the Rutherford County Historical Society*. In a document written many years after the war, Dr. Eames claimed to have seen citizens of Murfreesboro killing a number of African Americans who had been friendly with the U.S. troops. This account contradicts his own letter to his wife, which tells of being sick and seeing little of the actual attack on July 13, 1862. Also, his claims are not supported by any other U.S. witnesses.
17. Dr. Albert Wedge Speech, *Publications of the Rutherford County Historical Society*.
18. *Daily Union*, July 19, 1862.
19. Womack Collection, Civil War Sub-Group, Harding Letters, Box 18, Folder 228.
20. Carney, *Diary*, July 20, 1862.
21. William Eames to his wife, August 9, 1862.

CHAPTER 4

1. Spence, *Diary*, 50.
2. Carney, *Diary*, July 17, 18, 19, 21, 1862.
3. French, *Journal*, October 7, 1862. Smith had just heard of the death of Nelson.
4. King, *Memoirs*, Box 7, Folder 14, James M. King Collection, Albert Gore Research Center.
5. Ibid.
6. Spence, *Diary*, 51.

7. Charles W. Anderson, "War Experiences," *Confederate Veteran Magazine* 18 (1910): 8.

8. *OR*, ser. 1, vol. 20, pt. 1, 64.

9. Parks, *General Leonidas Polk*, 282.

10. West, *President Is Coming*, rutherfordhistory.org.

11. Neff and Pollitz, *Bride and the Bandit*, 62.

12. Ibid., 70.

13. Ibid., 62.

14. Ibid., 70–71.

15. Ramage, *Rebel Raider*, 58.

16. Ibid., 38.

17. Ibid., 63.

18. Personal interview with Mrs. Samuel Gilreath, Lebanon, Tennessee, granddaughter of Martha Ready Morgan Williamson, June 4, 1985.

19. Neff and Pollitz, *Bride and the Bandit*, 173.

20. Ibid., 186.

21. Memoirs of General Basil W. Duke, interview with *News-Banner* reporter, Louisville, Kentucky, August 31, 1912.

22. Neff and Pollitz, *Bride and the Bandit*, 199.

23. Pittard, *History of Rutherford County*, 73.

24. Shirley Farris Jones, "Martha Ready Morgan: From Wife to Widow in 630 Days," paper presented at Cumberland Valley Civil War Heritage Region Symposium, September 13, 2002.

25. Spence, *Diary*, 58–59.

26. *Daily Rebel Banner*, January 1, 1863, microfilm, Linebaugh Public Library.

27. Womack Collection, Civil War Sub-Group, Box 14, Folder 58, Miscellaneous Papers.

28. Fitch, *Annals of the Army*, 676–77.

29. Ridley, *Battles and Sketches*, 354.

30. Womack Collection, Civil War Sub-Group, Box 18, Folder 230, Miscellaneous Papers. Another entry in the account is dated March 12, 1863. It reads: "About 2 O'clock P.M. Deposited the case containing the remains of my dear son N.M. Bearden in the vault prepared for its reception in my garden. A large crowd of our friends and neighbors being present. He was in a wonderful state of preservation taking into consideration the length of time since his death. O how natural that manly brave and pleasant features did look to an all most broken hearted parent."

31. Spence, *Diary*, 62.

32. Jones, *Un-Civil War*, 54–55.
33. Ann Hosner letter, Sanitary Commission Folder, Archives of Stones River National Battlefield Park.
34. James King Moore Collection, Box 1, Folder 1; Bettie Ransom letter.

CHAPTER 5

1. Leonard E. Brown, "Fortress Rosecrans: A History," *Tennessee Historical Quarterly* 50, no. 3 (Fall 1991): 136–37.
2. Spence, *Diary*, 73.
3. Brown, "Fortress Rosecrans," 138.
4. Spence, *Diary*, 80; Mike West, "Union Army Destroyed Historic Church," *Murfreesboro Post*, October 4, 2011.
5. Milroy to his wife, May 5, 1864. Cited in Bradley, *With Blood and Fire*, xvi. The provost marshal records are separate from the *Official Records of the War of the Rebellion* and have generally been neglected by historians. These records show a widespread, persistent pattern of killing Southern civilians. This practice was known by Stanton and Lincoln since their signatures appear as endorsements on many of the orders issued to the officers who carried out the murders. The provost records are in the National Archives with microfilm copies (400 reels) in the Tennessee State Library and Archives.
6. Debra Glass and Heath Mathews, "Brigadier General Thomas Benton Smith, C.S.A," Civil War's Western Theater, http://armyoftennessee. wordpress.com/brigadier-general-thomas-benton-smith-c-s-a.
7. Allen Sullivan, "Gen. Thomas Benton Smith," 20th Tennessee Infantry Regiments, http://tennessee-scv.org/Camp854/tbsmith.htm.
8. Ibid.
9. Ibid.
10. Hugh F. Walker, "The Devotion and Death of DeWitt Jobe," *Blue and Gray Magazine* (April–May 1986): 44.
11. Pittard, *Legends and Stories*; *Publications of the Rutherford County Historical Society* 25 (Summer 1985): 40.
12. *Publications of the Rutherford County Historical Society* 25 (Summer 1985): 44.
13. Ibid., 48.
14. Mike West, "CSA Scout DeWitt Jobe Died Horrible Death," *Murfreesboro Post*, October 8, 2007. Quote from Ed Huddleston in "The Civil War in Middle Tennessee."

15. Pittard, *Legends and Stories*, 55.

16. Even firsthand accounts and newspaper articles are often based on invalid sources; for example, Bromfield Ridley's account in *Battles and Sketches of the Army of Tennessee*, where he states, "When he was told of Jobe's torture and persecution he grew desperate and his mind became unhinged. He left the 45th Tennessee Regiment near Chattanooga, raised the black flag, and declared that henceforth that he would never take a prisoner." At the time of Jobe's death, late August 1864, the Army of Tennessee was defending Atlanta. Smith left the 45th in September 1863, a year before Jobe was killed.

17. Spence, *Diary*, 150.

18. Pittard, *Legends and Stories*, 54.

19. Ibid., 151.

20. Van Zelm, "Hope Within a Wilderness of Suffering," 1.

21. *OR*, ser. 1, vol. 32, pt. 2, 269.

22. "Stones River National Cemetery," folder in the archives of Stones River National Battlefield.

23. Fraley, *Politics of Memory*. The contrast between the solemn commemoration of the sacrifices of the U.S. dead and the joyous celebration of emancipation became quite marked and was a point of controversy between the white pro-Union crowds who came to the cemetery on Memorial Day and the local African American population who viewed the occasion as one of celebration and not commemoration of sacrifice.

24. W.A. Gardner to J.W. Stephens, June 18, 1897, letter in possession of authors.

25. Fraley, *Politics of Memory*, 116–17, 123. Confederate Circle has been improved and maintained by the efforts of the local camp of the Sons of Confederate Veterans, Camp #33.

26. Stones River National Battlefield Park draws thousands of visitors to the town of Murfreesboro each year. The founding of the Battlefield Park was not a matter of controversy for a simple reason: national cemeteries *exclude* Confederates, but battlefield parks *include* them.

27. Union Provost Marshal Records, Microfilm Collection 416, Roll 50, TSLA.

28. King *Memoirs*, 79, Box 7, Folder 14, Gore Research Center.

29. Diary of F.E. Henderson, 1864; *Publications of the Rutherford County Historical Society* 10 (Winter 1978); Emma Lane Diary.

30. King, *Memoirs*, 79; RCHS, People Series, Box 1, Folder 7, Gore Research Center.

31. Diary of F.E. Henderson, 1864; *Publications of the Rutherford County Historical Society* 10 (Winter 1978).
32. King, *Memoirs*, 79.

CHAPTER 6

1. Debbie Chapman, "Civil War Notes," RCHS, 7.
2. Spence, *Diary*, 161.
3. Henderson, *Story of Murfreesboro*, 86.

APPENDIX

Sam Davis

1. Bethany Hawkins, "Confederate Hero Sam Davis," Reunion Booklet, Tennessee Division Reunion Sons of Confederate Veterans Military Order of the Stars and Bars, April 20, 21, 22, 2001, 24–26,
2. Peggy Robbins, "Samuel Davis." *Civil War: The Magazine of the Civil War Society* 8, no. 6, issue 26 (November–December 1990): 50–56.
3. Ibid.
4. Ibid.
5. Hawkins, "Confederate Hero."

William Ledbetter Jr.

1. Jonathan Fagan, "Rutherford Rifles Fire True," *Murfreesboro Post*, July 17, 2011, 15.
2. Henderson, *Story of Murfreesboro*, 84.
3. Fagan, "Rutherford Rifles."
4. Henry G. Wray, ed., "The Rutherford Rifles," *Publications of the Rutherford County Historical Society* 5 (Spring 1975): 43–44.
5. Mabel Pittard, "The Rutherford Rifles," *Publications of the Rutherford County Historical Society* 31 (Summer 1988):. 6.
6. Ibid.
7. Ibid.
8. Fagan, "Rutherford Rifles."
9. Ibid.

Joseph Palmer

1. Neff, *Tennessee's Battered Brigadier*. Comments from one of his associates, unidentified, in *Bench and Bar*, p. 354.
2. Ibid.
3. Ibid.
4. Ibid.
5. Henderson, *Story of Murfreesboro*.
6. Pittard, *Rutherford County*.
7. Neff, *Tennessee's Battered Brigadier*. Allisonia is a small community located near Tullahoma.
8. Ibid.
9. "Some Information about the Petitioners for Pardon," Confederate Amnesty Papers, Rutherford County Historical Society; *Fow Chips* 39, no. 2 (November/December 2009): 7.

Mary Kate Patterson

1. Marion Herndon Dunn, "The Unsinkable Mary Kate," http://tennessee-scv.org/Camp1293/unsinkable.htm.
2. "Samuel Davis' Sister-in-Law," *Confederate Veteran* 4 (February 1896), available online at http://tennessee-scv.org/colemanscouts/marykatecv.htm.
3. Ibid.
4. Ibid.
5. Ibid.

Bromfield Ridley Jr.

1. Ridley, *Battles and Sketches*, 149.
2. Ibid., 148.
3. Ibid., 354.
4. Ibid., 149.
5. Ibid., xi.
6. Ibid, prefatory note.

Bibliography

Allen, David C. *Winds of Change: Tennessee in the Civil War.* Nashville, TN: Land Yatch Press, 2000.

Beatty, John. *The Citizen Soldier.* Cincinnati, OH: Wilstack, Baldwin & Co., 1879.

Belt, Gordon, and Traci Nichols. *Onward Southern Soldiers.* Charleston, SC: The History Press, 2011.

Bergeron, Paul. *Papers of Andrew Johnson.* Knoxville: University of Tennessee Press, 1990.

Bradley, Michael R. *With Blood and Fire: Behind Union Lines in Middle Tennessee.* Shippensburg, PA.: Burd Street Press, 2003.

Carney, Kate. *Kate Carney Diary.* docsouth.unc.edu.

Duke, Basil Wilson. *History of Morgan's Cavalry.* Dayton, OH: Generals Books, 2009. Originally published, 1867.

Fitch, John. *Annals of the Army of the Cumberland.* Philadelphia: John Lippencott & Co., 1864.

Fraley, Miranda L. *Politics of Memory: Remembering the Civil War in Rutherford County Tennessee.* PhD diss. Indiana University, 2004. [Copy in archives of Stones River National Battlefield.]

French, Lucy Virginia. *Journal.* Edited by Jerry Smith. Privately printed, n.d.

Harding Letters. Womack Collection. Albert Gore Research Center, Middle Tennessee State University, Murfreesboro, TN.

Hatcher, Joe. "No Votes For Lincoln." Womack Collection, Albert Gore Research Center, Middle Tennessee State University, Murfreesboro, TN.

Henderson, C.C. *The Story of Murfreesboro*. Murfreesboro, TN: News-Banner Pub. Co., 1929. Reprint, Franklin Pub. Co., 1977.

Hughes, Mary B. *Hearthstones: The Story of Historic Rutherford County Homes.* Murfreesboro, TN: Mid-South Publishing Co., 1942.

Jones, Shirley Farris. *The Un-Civil War in Middle Tennessee.* Rutherford County Historical Society, 2010.

Jordan, Thomas, and J.P. Pryor. *The Campaigns of General Nathan Bedford Forrest and of Forrest's Cavalry.* New York: Da Capo Press, 1996. Original printing, 1868.

King, James Moore Collection. Albert Gore Research Center, Middle Tennessee State University.

Lane, Emma. *Diary.* RCHS Collections. People Series, Box 1, Folder 7. Albert Gore Research Center, Middle Tennessee State University.

McHenry, Robert, ed. *Webster's American Military Biographies.* Springfield, MA: G&C Merriam Co., 1978.

Neff, Robert O., and Edith E. Pollitz. *The Bride and the Bandit.* Evansville, IN: Evansville Bindery (privately printed), 1998.

———. *Tennessee's Battered Brigadier: The Life of General Joseph B. Palmer, CSA.* Franklin, TN: Hillsboro Press, 2000.

Official Records of the War of the Rebellion. Washington, D.C.: Government Printing Office, 1880–1901.

Parks, Joseph H. *General Leonidas Polk, CSA: The Fighting Bishop.* Baton Rouge: Louisiana State University Press, 1990.

Pittard, Mable. *History of Rutherford County.* Memphis, TN: Memphis State University Press, 1984.

———. *Legends and Stories of Civil War Rutherford County.* Master's thesis, George Peabody College for Teachers, August 1940.

Poole, James Randolph. *Cracker Cavaliers.* Macon, GA: Mercer University Press, 2000.

Ramage, James A. *Rebel Raider: The Life of General John Hunt Morgan.* Lexington: University of Kentucky Press, 1986.

Ready, Alice. Journal. Unpublished. Southern Historical Collection, Chapel Hill, NC. [Original given by Mrs. Mary Martin Brown.]

Ridley, Bromfield. *Battles and Sketches of the Army of Tennessee.* Dayton, OH: Morningside House, 1995. Originally published, 1906.

Rutherford County Historical Society Collection. Albert Gore Research Center, Middle Tennessee State University, Murfreesboro, TN.

Stones River National Cemetery. Folder in Archives of Stones River National Battlefield.

Union Provost Marshal Records. MC 345 and MC 416, Tennessee State Library and Archives.

Van Zelm, Antoinette. "Hope Within a Wilderness of Suffering." Tennessee Civil War National Heritage Area publication.

Wharton, G.W., to Daniel Weeden. Womack Collection. Albert Gore Research Center, Middle Tennessee State University, Murfreesboro, TN.

Wilson, Sadye Tune, Nancy Tune Fitzgerald and Richard Warwick, eds. *Letters to Laura: A Confederate Surgeon's Impressions of Four Years of War.* Nashville, TN: Tunstede, 1996.

Wyeth, John Allan. *That Devil Forrest.* Baton Rouge: Louisiana State University Press, 1989. First published, 1899.

About the Authors

Michael R. Bradley earned his PhD from Vanderbilt University and taught U.S. history for thirty-six years at Motlow College in Tullahoma, Tennessee. Now professor emeritus, he remains an active author and speaker. He has written a number of Civil War books, including *Forrest's Fighting Preacher: David Campbell Kelley of Tennessee*, also published by The History Press. Dr. Bradley is a life member of the Sons of Confederate Veterans and is the immediate past commander of the Tennessee Division of SCV. He and his wife live in Tullahoma, Tennessee.

Shirley Farris Jones is a lifelong resident of Murfreesboro. A graduate of Knox Business College, she is a Civil War historian and community activist, retired from Middle Tennessee State University, where she had been a staff member for more than thirty years. Shirley is a founding member of the Middle Tennessee Civil War Round Table and a former president of the Rutherford County Historical Society, the Rutherford County Chapter of the Association for the Preservation of Tennessee Antiquities, the Friends of Stones River National Battlefield and the Martha Ready Morgan Chapter of the United Daughters of the Confederacy. Shirley has written three other books, including *The Un-Civil War in Middle Tennessee*, and numerous Civil War–related articles. She and her husband live in Murfreesboro, Tennessee.

www.ingramcontent.com/pod-product-compliance
Lightning Source LLC
Chambersburg PA
CBHW060810100426
42813CB00004B/1023